#Thisiswhatticklesme

Khaled M. Ismail

#Thisiswhatticklesme
Copyright © 2019 Khaled M. Ismail
First published in 2019

ISBN
Paperback: 978-0-6485050-9-9
E-book: 978-0-6486663-0-1

All rights reserved. No part of this book may be reproduced, stored in a retrieval system, or transmitted by any means (electronic, mechanical, photocopying, recording, or otherwise) without written permission from the author.

Because of the dynamic nature of the internet, any web addresses or links contained in this book may have changed since publication and may no longer be valid. The information in this book is based on the author's experiences and opinions. The views expressed in this book are solely those of the author and do not necessarily reflect the views of the publisher; the publisher hereby disclaims any responsibility for them.

The author of this book does not dispense any form of medical, legal, financial, or technical advice either directly or indirectly. The intent of the author is solely to provide information of a general nature to help you in your quest for personal development and growth. In the event, you use any of the information in this book, the author and the publisher assume no responsibility for your actions. If any form of expert assistance is required, the services of a competent professional should be sought.

Publishing information
Publishing, design, and production facilitated by
Passionpreneur Publishing
www.PassionpreneurPublishing.com

Melbourne, Victoria Australia

Dedication

This book is dedicated to my family who have encouraged and challenged me from the beginning and every day.

To my wife Janice Adey
My daughter Samantha Ismail
My son Bradley Ismail

I have tickled you way too many times during the writing of every story, post, and, eventually, this book.

You were my compass.

Thank you.

Acknowledgement

I wish to acknowledge with gratitude all my contacts on LinkedIn who have supported me with their enlightening comments and positive engagement on every post for the past couple of years.

. . . and I wish to especially acknowledge my wonderful friends and colleagues who have inspired me to continue to write, critiqued my tickling ideas and thoughts, proof read my posts, and endured with me throughout.

Introduction

#Thisiswhatticklesme

This is not a traditional self-help book that will help you become a multimillionaire or make you fall asleep. This is actually an anti-book disguised in book format.

This book is entertaining, informative, and educational. So, there is a little bit of fun and many *aha* moments. I have put this together based on the many posts I have on LinkedIn, which I still write today in a mini-blog format.

Many of the posts are from my everyday life experiences and observations at work and during my many travels, and from interacting with interesting people. It is a modern version of a personal diary, but with a purpose.

The title of the book and my many posts are self-explanatory – #Thisiswhatticklesme – which is about things which annoy me a little or a lot and about things that make me think!

I am not your typical corporate executive with 30 years of experience in multinational companies, as I constantly try to find ways to reinvent myself. I am now a serial investor in various sectors, and you will next find me flipping gourmet burgers and serving fine wine in my beachfront restaurant, somewhere where the sun is shining.

I hope you enjoy reading this book as much as I enjoyed writing each post.

I wonder what tickles you? (See last page.)

Post # 1

Cucumbers, potatoes, T-shirts, and belts per kilo

#Thisiswhatticklesme

The man outside the shop sounded like he was selling cucumbers or potatoes by the kilo at a discount . . . but he wasn't!

I had to take a second look. It was a clothing store, not a grocery or a butcher's shop.

The sign read 'Vintage per kilo! €15/kg'

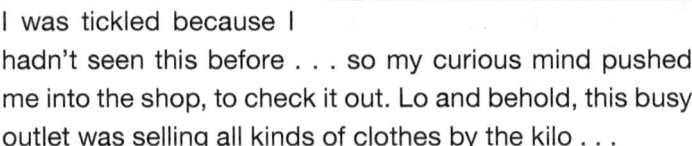

I was tickled because I hadn't seen this before . . . so my curious mind pushed me into the shop, to check it out. Lo and behold, this busy outlet was selling all kinds of clothes by the kilo . . .

I picked up a couple of items:

- one vintage T-shirt
- one colourful jacket fit for a rock star
- one tie from the 70s, and
- one green belt

And went to the weighing machine . . .

They weighed 0.94 kg.

The lady next to me whispered, 'Add a scarf to reach 1 kg.'

Wow! All this for €15! (US$16.94.)

I learnt that this is a new phenomenon, which started a little over 10 years ago in pop-up shops, during the last financial crisis. Wholesalers would buy 10,000–20,000 kg of used clothes from retailers and other fashion houses and sell them at these 'Vintage per kilo' shops (otherwise they could end up in landfills—yes, the garbage). What a great way to reuse/recycle!

Thankfully, and to spare my daughter from embarrassment, they only took 'cash', and I only had a credit card. Maybe next time . . .

Would you buy 'Vintage per kilo'?

Post # 2

Six Bach pieces for US$32 on a US$3.5 million violin

#Thisiswhatticklesme

True story . . . A man sat in a metro station in Washington, DC, and started to play the violin; he played six Bach pieces for 45 min and collected US$32 in tips. When he finished playing and silence took over, no one noticed. No one applauded, nor was there any recognition.

The violinist was Joshua Bell, one of the best musicians in the world. He played one of the most intricate pieces ever written, with a violin worth US$3.5 million!

Two days ago, Joshua Bell sold out at a theatre in Boston, and the seats averaged US$100 each. Tickling, isn't it?

This was a social experiment organised by the *Washington Post* about perception, taste, and the priorities of people.

Conclusion: Do we appreciate beauty and talent in the wrong place and in an unexpected context?

I am no *Washington Post*, and this guitarist in the picture is no Joshua Bell . . . but . . . I noticed him, and he made my day with his music.

So, the question is this: If we do not take a moment to stop and listen to one of the best musicians in the world playing the best music ever written, how many other things are we missing?

Post # 3

Don't pick your nose in public

#Thisiswhatticklesme

I was thrilled to be leaving the scorching heat (49°C) in Dubai for meetings in Europe . . . my luck . . . Europe was experiencing a heat wave, and air conditioners were scarce!

My excitement was subdued when I saw my fellow passenger navigating the on-board entertainment system with his smelly feet!

As you can imagine, this tickled me with a capital T!

I gave him 'the look'!

This made me reflect on 10 etiquettes I've learnt and that I practise (most of the time).

1. Open the door for the person behind you (regardless of gender).
2. Let people get off the elevator first before you barge in.
3. Don't pick your nose or clip your nails in public.
4. When talking to someone in person, don't constantly glance down at your phone or answer messages or e-mails.
5. If you leave your phone on your desk, put it on the silent mode.
6. Say 'Please' and 'Thank you'.
7. When you call someone, always ask if now is a good time to talk.
8. If you say, 'I invite you', that means *you* pay.
9. If your office has 'Casual Thursdays or Fridays', don't dress like you're going to the beach. And . . .
10. Don't use your feet to navigate a touchscreen in a public place!

What's your favourite etiquette?

Post # 4

Things that make me proud

#Thisiswhatticklesme

People change . . . I changed. I am no longer the same person I was 25 or 30 years ago. I remember what used to make me happy and proud then.

Top five things that made me happy/proud back then:

1. Being praised for doing a good job
2. Getting a raise or a promotion
3. Buying my first car
4. Renting my own apartment
5. Meeting a girl (now wife!)

Don't get me wrong; these are all wonderful things that we should be happy about and proud of.

But things change; now other things make me happy/proud:

1. Volunteering my time (giving back)
2. Writing a **#thisiswhatticklesme** post (sharing knowledge)
3. Giving other people a promotion or a raise
4. Defending or protecting others
5. Seeing my kids grow and achieve things. Today I am both super happy and proud to see my kids graduate from high school (son) and university (daughter)

What tickles me is that this also makes me feel 'mature', which is just a more sophisticated way of saying 'old'!

What makes you happy?

#prouddad

Post # 5

We The North

#Thisiswhatticklesme

It's not 1 July! Not yet. But something has been happening in the city from the moment I landed in Toronto to celebrate my daughter's graduation.

At the airport, I started noticing that there was a common theme/slogan being repeated: 'We The North'.

By the time I got into the car, I forgot all about it.

Then it appeared again on flags hanging from balconies and construction sites, on coffee cups and Instagram posts, and again on giant screens and store stickers in the middle of the city.

At dinner, I saw an older gentleman with a giant button pinned to his sweater.

'What is going on?' I asked myself. I am used to this euphoria and sense of unity around 1 July in Canada, but Canada Day was a couple of weeks away.

Khaled M. Ismail

It tickled me how three simple, confident, and unapologetic words gave a country a renewed sense of pride . . . a sense of identity (besides super-nice people and maple syrup).

This is a campaign slogan that started five years ago for a basketball team (Raptors – the only NBA team in Canada), which was now uniting a nation.

Can a slogan unite a company, a team, a nation?

#wethenorth

Post # 6

Oh no! She is crying

#Thisiswhatticklesme

I was watching Theresa May's speech with interest, as I have been following the Brexit drama for a long time . . . 'Oh wait . . . she just resigned . . . Oh no . . . she is crying!'

'Here is a leader (like her or not) who is showing genuine emotion – as she has nothing to gain or lose at this point,' I reflected!

I have heard the phrase 'Not a career enhancing move!' several times before . . . when someone says or does something unusual or outside the norm.

PS. 'Norms' may change from one – company, country, or culture – to another.

The real question, though, is this: Is it OK to show emotion at work? Anger, shouting, crying, etc. . . . .

Khaled M. Ismail

Who would you rather work with?

1. A stable flatliner – one who shows no emotion, regardless of the situation?
2. Someone who wears their heart on their sleeve?

1 or 2?

Post # 7

Are you good at Math?

A Lady walks into a store and steals a €100 bill from the register without the owner's knowledge. She comes back five minutes later and buys €70 worth of goods with the €100 bill she stole. The owner gives her €30 in change.

How much did the owner lose?
A. €30   B. €70   C. €100
D. €130   E. €170   F. €200

#Thisiswhatticklesme

'Are you good at math?' I asked.

'But, of course!' replied a seasoned CFO, and a private banker nodded!

I was having dinner with both (friends), and it tickled me that they were both rubbish at either math or logic, and they contradicted each other trying to solve the question above.

Khaled M. Ismail

I found this post on social media, and it became the subject of our dinner, even continued into dessert!

How's your math?

How much did the owner lose?

PS. Wanted: A private banker!

Post # 8

Invest in what?

#Thisiswhatticklesme

I was sitting and discussing investment ideas and strategies with my banker friends . . . suddenly a 'fashionista', an acquaintance of ours, who was eavesdropping, stuck her nose in and said, 'Birkin! Buy a couple of Birkins and sit on them!'

'Is that a stock or an IPO, or are you talking about the handbags?' I asked.

She rolled her eyes. 'Birkin handbags, darrrling! You know, by Hermès ?' she answered and swiftly walked away for a selfie with a friend. I thought she was nuts! Until . . .

I learned more about the genius behind Hermès's marketing strategy: 'Make something rare . . . so rare that you can't easily buy it and see what happens.' Hermès controls and limits the number of bags produced each year. The bags are never advertised anywhere, to maintain their exclusivity; it is next to impossible to buy a Birkin bag directly from a Hermès store or boutique, and you're lucky if you get your hands on this iconic handbag. What tickles me is that since the launch of the Birkin bag, the price has risen by an average of 14 per cent per year, outperforming traditional investments such as the S&P 500 and gold markets.

Note to self: Change investment portfolio!

PS. A Birkin handbag, second-hand, can be worth US$135,000 or more. I know it is a little over the top (OTT), but raise your hand if you think it is worth it anyway!

Post # 9

Burj Khalifa without elevators?

#Thisiswhatticklesme

'Data is the new oil' is a phrase I've heard way too many times for my liking. I see where the analogy comes from (they both need to be refined to be super useful), but I disagree.

I reflected for a while, and it hit me when I was driving by Burj Khalifa – the tallest building in the world. So, imagine Burj Khalifa is the 'Cloud' (a large data centre), and each floor (of its 200 floors) is a data 'Edge' centre (which brings data closer to the user to speed up transactions), and let's imagine the elevators are the 'Connectivity'.

Can we agree that Burj Khalifa without elevators would be a beautiful but useless structure?

And with painfully slow elevators, Burj Khalifa would be tickling at best for its tenants and visitors.

Khaled M. Ismail

Now imagine the fastest elevators in the world with a speed of 36 km/h or 600m/min or 10m/s transporting people to its different floors. Now we are talking business! I think 'Connectivity' – and more specifically, its speed – is the new gold . . . to our goldfish attention–span culture.

Are we on the same wavelength?

Post # 10

The brief: make kale cool

#Thisiswhatticklesme

I paid US$24 for a kale salad yesterday! Ouch! Usually, salad is the more reasonably priced item on restaurant menus – but not kale, which is now positioned as a superfood and has achieved a mighty pop culture–icon status, unlike her poor sisters – spinach, cabbage, bok choy, and brussels sprouts (with similar nutritional value).

I had never heard of kale until about five years ago! It tickled me, and I wondered where the craze about this fibrous and bitter salad bar garnish came from, and who was behind it.

I found the answer: 'The power of PR with a high dosage of contacts and celebrity involvement.' In 2013, Oberon Sinclair, founder of My Young Auntie PR agency in New York City, was briefed by the American Kale Association to 'make kale cool', and a couple of years later . . . the rest is history . . . and we now even have 'National Kale Day'

Khaled M. Ismail

on 1 October! This proves that savvy marketing and PR can not only form trends but also sway our food choices.

Do you even like kale?

Post # 11

Sh!

#Thisiswhatticklesme

'You got a minute?' or 'Have you heard?' is usually the beginning of a juicy story or news.

There have been so many times I've been told a confidential piece of information (a.k.a. a 'secret') by one person and then got to hear it again from another! Has that happened to you?

Let me demonstrate:

10:05 AM – A colleague walks into your office tiptoeing like a thief and says, 'Have you heard? Roman has been fired! But keep it to yourself.'

10:30 AM – By the coffee machine another person, looking over his shoulder, says, 'Hmm, not sure if I should tell you, but Roman got the sack.' It tickles me . . . but you've got to smile!

Khaled M. Ismail

In the dictionary, a secret is defined as 'Something that is kept or meant to be kept unknown or unseen by others.'

In real life and my definition of a secret is 'Something juicy that you tell one person at a time!' Are you a culprit? Have you ever told a secret?

Sh, I won't tell anyone!

Post # 12

Free body massage!

#Thisiswhatticklesme

After a week of meetings, strategy discussions, learning new jargon, and negotiating budgets, I was happy to be travelling home . . . until I arrived at the airport and saw the length of the zigzag security line.

I know it is for my 'safety', but it was certainly not fun waiting in that long queue and going through the usual tickling security routine:

- Taking my jacket off
- Emptying my pocket – out goes my phone
- Removing all liquids from my bag and placing them in a plastic bag as instructed
- Throwing away an almost empty deodorant bottle that was 125 ml (Oh . . . 25 ml over the limit!)
- Computer and iPad out, and removing my watch
- Whipping out my belt and . . . I had to go back and take my shoes off

Khaled M. Ismail

I still buzzed. So, I was given a very thorough pat down! (Which I now call a free massage). It got me thinking, 'What got us to this level of scrutiny and why?'

I Googled and discovered that before 1972 none of this scrutiny existed. Between 1968 and 1972, hijackers discovered this flying fuselage and got busy threatening people left, right, and centre. In response, the FAA required airports to screen all passengers and their carry-on bags from 5 January 1973.

What will they do next? Will they require *all* passengers to shower before boarding? Hmm, not a bad idea!

Post # 13

Are you an expat or an immigrant?

#Thisiswhatticklesme

MK came to Dubai in 2000 to work for two years, and he is still here . . . living, running his own business and thriving. I called him an 'immigrant'. He said that he would classify himself as an 'expat'. We debated the difference!

Dictionary

An 'expatriate' (often shortened to expat) is a person temporarily or permanently residing in a country other than their native country.

An 'immigrant' is a person who comes to live temporarily or permanently in a foreign country.

Hmm, the definitions are ticklingly similar. Who is an immigrant and who is an expat?

- A Ukrainian plumber living and working in London
- A Turkish taxi company owner living and working in Munich
- A Swiss businesswoman living and working in Shanghai
- An Ethiopian medical professional living and working at a hospital in Paris
- A British salesman living and working in Cairo
- A Syrian professor working in Stockholm as a janitor (waiting to return to his homeland once it becomes safe again)

According to the above definition, all these people should be defined as ????? because they are living outside their birth country for an undefined period of time.

IMHO both terms are loaded. They carry many connotations, preconceptions, and assumptions about race, class, education, and privilege. Are you an expat or an immigrant?

Post # 14

Diversity and inclusion

Diversity is what you have and inclusion is what you do!

#Thisiswhatticklesme

I am not the brightest light bulb, so I like to break down and simplify things to understand them. The buzz word on the street and in most companies now is not just 'Diversity' but also 'Inclusion'.

We sometimes tend to complicate and overengineer concepts to look smart, and adding complex words, graphs, and KPIs around them, without simplifying them, doesn't always help.

I get why 'diversity' is super important in any successful workplace, but where did the word 'inclusion' come from?

It tickled me, so I wanted to make it easy for my simple brain, and I finally found the definition I understood: Diversity often focuses on the differences and is referred to as 'the mix'.

Khaled M. Ismail

Inclusion is the deliberate act of welcoming diversity and creating an environment where all different kinds of people can thrive and succeed.

So . . . 'diversity' is what you have, and 'inclusion' is what you do.

Agree?

Post # 15

Catfight in space

#Thisiswhatticklesme

So, there I was being a geek this morning reading and watching videos about satellites, speed, and internet connectivity.

SpaceX (Elon Musk) and Amazon (Jeff Bezos) are having a catfight about who is going to be first and who is copying from whom! SpaceX plans to launch a 4,425-satellite constellation, and Amazon plans to launch a 3,236-satellite constellation to provide global, high-speed, reliable, and affordable internet access.

Space will be so congested that you won't be able to distinguish between stars and satellites.

Frankly, I don't care! I just want to be able to check my e-mails and send my mother a picture of me in front of the Eiffel Tower for less than the cost of a fancy five-course meal on the Champs-Élysées.

Khaled M. Ismail

Roaming charges are so prohibitively expensive! What tickles me is how far we've come . . . I will soon be able to send my friend Bruce in Johannesburg a picture of my lunch in Paris in the 'blink of an eye' – in specifically 90 milliseconds (that's 0.09 s).

What's next?

Post # 16

Policy

I have policies too!

#Thisiswhatticklesme

'This is not our company policy, sir,' the service manager repeated three times, in a firm way, to three different legitimate requests, which I raised from a long-winded contract filled with 'fine print' that protects them against every eventuality.

One of them tickled me.

It stated that they will deduct US$150 as 'administration fee' if I decide to cancel my 'fully paid annual' service contract due to their negligence . . .

Yes . . . if *they* made a mistake and I decide to cancel the contract, they will deduct US$150 from the balance they owe me.

I counted to 10 and calmly responded, 'I will not pay any admin fee, and that is *my* policy . . . oh . . . and it is also my policy not to accept the other two clauses.' I continued, 'Please amend the contract accordingly and resend it or let's not waste each other's time . . . please, and thank you.'

Note to service providers: Consumers have choices and policies too!

They may not be written anywhere, but they exist in our heads.

Was my response reasonable? Well . . .

PS. The contract was amended, and we lived happily ever after!

Post # 17

Oh no, not you again!

#Thisiswhatticklesme

I can't live without it. It is happy. It is contagious. It breaks barriers and opens doors both in everyday life and in business.

Yes, I am talking about humour! Without it, life can be a little dry and, sometimes, tasteless. If you don't have a sense of humour, I feel that you are not using your full potential to connect with people. Humour comes in all sorts of 'shapes and sizes'.

Some are 'in your face', some are 'dry', and some are 'self-deprecating'.

Each culture has some, even though you might not think so at first, or you may not even understand it.

If you are not careful, some humour could offend people, but some is simply universal. Recently, at a flea market, I was tickled when a friend of mine said, 'Hmm, I wouldn't feel too welcome going to someone's house with this doormat.' The doormat had 'Oh no, not you again' written on it.

I went straightaway and bought it and said, 'Exactly why I want it, if it makes you come over less often!'

I thought it was hilarious. We both laughed and walked into the sunset, with the doormat in hand.

Post # 18

Never make fun of someone who speaks broken English. It means they know another language!

#Thisiswhatticklesme

She was young, petite, timid, and had a 'foreign' name. I met her at one of our company events where we had more than 30 nationalities and an equal number of languages represented.

I knew of her, but I didn't know her well, so I didn't pay too much attention . . . until I found out that she spoke seven languages fluently!

It tickled me!

But what really tickled me was how she 'worked the room' at the evening cocktail. She managed to make friends with almost everyone, especially when they knew that she spoke their language or at least knew how to say the usual 'hello', 'thank you', and 'bad' words!

My late father once told me, 'Every language you know opens up a multitude of opportunities for you.'

How many languages do *you* speak?

Post # 19

80 per cent . . .

And you call that diversity?

#Thisiswhatticklesme

I did the math this morning, and the diversity on my team doesn't look that great, to be honest! 80 per cent of my team members are women! You would be a little disappointed when you find out that the diversity numbers on your team are significantly skewed one way or the other.

Well, I wasn't, and I am not . . .

For me, business is business, and if you make me proud of our achievements, talent and commitment supersede gender.

What tickles me (in a nice way) is that women have contributed considerably to my career growth, and they are the ones who continue to deliver and shine.

To them, I say, 'Happy Women's Day, today and every day!'

Post # 20

Would you tell him?

#Thisiswhatticklesme

Am I morally obliged to tell him?

A long-time friend – let's call him Joe – just accepted an offer to work for Company X.

Joe was really excited to take on the job, as he had been unemployed for some time.

I was told by someone who works for Company X that Joe's offer was 30 per cent lower than another candidate who had just accepted an identical position.

Both candidates have the exact same experience (but are from different nationalities).

What tickled me was how awkward I felt contemplating telling him what I know. I just didn't want to ruin his excitement . . .

Would you tell him?

Post # 21

What was the brief?

#Thisiswhatticklesme

Scene 1: 'I am so frustrated with my agency; they don't get it. I think I am going to look for another one,' said a client friend of mine.

Scene 2: 'My client doesn't know what he wants, and we are wasting so much time and effort; we are losing money. We may, unfortunately, have to resign the account,' said an agency friend of mine.

Coincidentally they were talking about each other (separately).

I asked my agency friend, 'What was the brief?'

He said, 'They asked us to make an impactful digital campaign for product X that will go viral.' (Response shortened so I don't bore you to death)

'That's it?' I asked.

'Yes,' the agency friend replied.

'And you accepted that brief?' I asked incredulously.

'Yes, we needed the job,' the agency friend replied.

I sent a group WhatsApp message to both of them with the words "Garbage in, garbage out" and exited the group!

I think they both got the message.

I later learnt that they continued to work together.

The end

Post # 22

Common sense, or is it?

#Thisiswhatticklesme

'Common sense' is not so common anymore. Today, obvious things need to be explained. 'Legal' must be consulted, focus groups need to be conducted, business cases need to be made with justification and substantiation, and don't forget the consultants . . . ah . . . and does it offend anyone?

This is now the modus operandi of all brand managers and marketers before they launch or promote any product.

A supermarket sign on a pile of peanuts read:

'This product contains peanuts'

Really!

All along I thought it contained kiwi puree!

But the winner is a warning sign on a high-power electricity cabinet: 'DO NOT TOUCH – Not only will this kill you, but it will also hurt the whole time you are dying'.

I thought it would just tickle a little.

Post # 23

How lazy are we?

#Thisiswhatticklesme

I would like to meet that consumer who buys peeled mandarins, just to learn more about his/her motives.

Is that consumer looking for convenience? Really?

How difficult is it to peel a mandarin? It's not even cut into nice little peeled pieces like I like them.

How busy or lazy is that consumer?

Those products tickle me and make me wonder what next.

But . . . I see a business opportunity here to launch the following services for such consumers:

- 'Poor baby' – Nose blowing service
- 'Stand still' – Shoelace tying service
- 'Open wide' – Feeding service

I welcome your ideas on any additional required services.

Post # 24

Repeat, repeat!

#Thisiswhatticklesme

Hear me out! This is tried and tested. A little while back, I decided to say and repeat the words:

'I am going to have a good day' . . . from the moment I wake up and throughout the day, and especially when I encounter a tickling person or situation.

I discovered that 9 out of 10 times, I end up having an awesome day.

It works; I encourage you to try it.

What tickles me is that I found that it doesn't work as well when I say and repeat, 'I am going to win US$1 million today.'

PS. I even tried saying it in different languages.

Post # 25

How many weekends do you have left?

#Thisiswhatticklesme

This weekend, I was having a heated discussion with a couple of good friends – not about politics or religion, but about personal values – and we had a difference of opinion.

Our third friend was listening quietly with a smirk on his face for the longest time, and then he suddenly interrupted us with, 'Do you wanna know how many weekends you have left?'

We looked at him with raised eyebrows!!!

'I saw this video online, and I can now calculate approximately how many weekends you have left and how many we have together,' he continued.

He did a rough calculation on his broken phone, and the results tickled me.

'C'mon, be nice to each other,' he concluded.

I dismissively told him, 'Go get that screen fixed! . . . do you know how many weekends *you* have left?'

But I silently agreed with him.

Post # 26

Just imagine!

#Thisiswhatticklesme

I had deep nail marks on my arm from my sister-in-law after we landed. She has an extreme fear of heights!

At 13, I had a mild and tickling fear of heights. My boarding school was on a mountain (altitude 1,300 m) overlooking a valley. The school was so high that it was/is called 'Beau Soleil' (Beautiful Sun) because we were above the clouds most of the time.

I still remember what my teacher told me one day (about my fear of heights):

Just imagine how much more you'd be able to see and how much more you'd enjoy being here, if you learnt to overcome this fear.

I had an incentive! Those powerful words resurface, at intervals, for me today.

Khaled M. Ismail

What tickles me is that I now get a kick out of flying and out of heights.

So 'just imagine' that you now like the sound of fingernails scratching on a chalkboard . . .

Post # 27

'There are two rules for success . . .
Rule # 1: Never reveal everything you know
Rule # 2: "   " '

#Thisiswhatticklesme

In my downtime, I like to read printed business articles, cases, and biographies – both online and offline . . . sometimes I discretely scan through some glossy and gossip titles. I do that to expand my knowledge so I can be successful.

I occasionally stumble upon some thought-provoking quotes . . . like this one.

This quote tickled me because the author (Roger) got distracted and did not finish his thought.

What is the second rule?

Post # 28

The most anticlimactic day!

#Thisiswhatticklesme

I think New Year's Eve (NYE) is the most anticlimactic day of the year, but I still love it!

Anticlimactic because there is so much hype, the frenzy of planning that goes into it, the many e-mails and messages about where you could or should go to celebrate NYE, and the exorbitant prices . . .

Then midnight comes and goes, and by 12:15 AM (after the screaming, fireworks, and hugging), if you are still awake, sober, or conscious, you think to yourself:

'That's it? It's all finished?' or 'Oh look, I didn't turn into a pumpkin!'

And I love it because it symbolically and literally closes one chapter and opens another exciting one. Here is to a brave, marvellous, and another tickling New Year.

Post # 29

Do you have the 'weird week'?

#Thisiswhatticklesme

I am usually in control most of the year! I know what I am doing (most of the time), where I am going, and when, until the last week of the year rolls in!

The period between Christmas and New Year tickles me! I call it the 'weird week'!

I am always asking myself and others what day it is. I go to sleep and wake up at strange hours . . .

Is it just me?

Besides spending time with family, I spend time staring at the wall (sometimes the ceiling) reflecting about the year gone by and what the next one may hold!

What do you do during this 'weird week'?

Post # 30

The 3 Cs
And how thick is your mattress?

#Thisiswhatticklesme

We all have one. Some work very hard to build and protect theirs, others don't as much!

You guessed it! It's your personal brand or company's reputation.

What people say about you when you are not in the room... is your reputation.

Think of your reputation as a mattress . . . the thicker the mattress, the softer the fall and more importantly, the greater the bounce back.

In a recent interview, I talked about the 3 Cs of reputation and crisis management and how to make that mattress thicker.

#Thisiswhatticklesme

Mainly from a corporate perspective, but most of it applies to individuals also – you and I are brands too.

I wonder what people say about me when 'I am not in the room'. It tickles me!

Post # 31

I thought I was going for lunch

#Thisiswhatticklesme

My daughter said that we were going for lunch. I have been talking to her about being brave and going outside her comfort zone!!!

She knew skydiving was outside my comfort zone, so she tricked me and decided I was going to play Santa from

#Thisiswhatticklesme

13,000 ft (but without the sleigh or the presents), and be brave.

What tickled me was that seconds before 'the jump' I was questioning my judgement, but Linley didn't let me finish my thoughts.

This is my brave story, what's yours?

Merry Christmas to all those who are celebrating.

#brave

Post # 32

Panel discussions Audience: ZZZZZZZ

#Thisiswhatticklesme

In all small and big conferences, we expect audience engagement, and we constantly try to get them involved! Surely, we don't want them to fall asleep.

At a recent conference, the moderator and my co-panellists were simply *awesome* trying to discuss an important topic, but I am not sure if all in the audience were fully conscious.

When we started our panel discussion (our 'private' chat on stage), some audience members pulled out their mobile phones for a quick e-mail check, others started dinner plans, and some fell asleep . . .

And I don't blame them!

On a serious and reflective note, I think that the panel discussion format – in all events and conferences, no matter the topic – needs to evolve/change to include and involve the audience more.

Agree?

Suggestions?

Post # 33

Know your worth – you must find the courage to leave the table if respect is no longer being served.

—**Tene Edwards**

#Thisiswhatticklesme

I was searching for an easy read to quench my thirst for knowledge, and I stumbled upon this author whom I'd never heard of: Tene Edwards

I am not a fan of motivational quotes, but this one got my attention, and I subscribe to it. Do you?

Post # 34

I will argue with anyone about anything!

#Thisiswhatticklesme

Some people like to have their presence known – 'occupy space'; others simply like to hear themselves talk – 'share of voice'. And some just like to argue – argue about a company policy, a word in a PowerPoint presentation, or the colour of water.

I am sure you have a colleague or a friend who likes to argue about everything and nothing.

These people are entertaining, but they can sometimes tickle you!

When someone wants to start an argument with me, I quickly ask myself:

1. Is it worth it?
2. What do I stand to gain?
3. Will winning the argument win me a trophy?

Khaled M. Ismail

Like . . .

Should people be allowed to put pineapple on pizza?

Post # 35

No working during drinking hours!

#Thisiswhatticklesme

Things have been splendidly busy lately. Like most of you, I have been occupied with work, travel, meetings, conferences, endless calls . . . you know, the usual.

I decided to go out and 'let my hair down' a little (whatever is left of it). I arrived at this place where the music was blazing and the ambience was hip and cool.

I settled down and started to look at the menu, sneaking a sporadic look at my phone with every notification and occasionally picking it up to view or answer (a very bad habit, I know).

I raised my head, and I saw this sign in my face – *'No working during drinking hours'*. I silently giggled to myself.

I thought, 'No more work for the night . . . because I am a law-abiding citizen,' and I didn't want to break that establishment's rules or policies!

How many times do you pick up your phone/day?

(No need to guess . . . if you have an iPhone, go to Settings, Screen Time, et voila!)

The number I saw on my phone tickled me!

Post # 36

I didn't know what algorithm meant!

#Thisiswhatticklesme

I felt inadequate! Four years ago, I felt left out. The digital world was passing me by 100 miles/s.

I didn't know what algorithm meant, and at first, I thought it was someone's funny name.

I didn't know what SEO stood for. I thought it was someone's fancy title. I didn't know what any of these terms really, really meant:

- Scaling and MAU (essential for valuation)
- Gamification (addiction)
- Deep links
- Geolocation and geotargeting (creepy)
- Notifications (annoying, but super important)
- UGC, CTR, SEM, #, UX/UI
- Ephemeral content
- Metadata

- Native and hybrid apps
- Organic reach, etc., etc., etc. . . . .
- And, dare I say . . . tokens, bitcoin AI, and blockchain

Now I know all of the above and a little more (I think), through a very tickling process . . . thanks to a CRAZY idea to start a global vlogging social media app called 1TAM, with two other partners and an awesome developer team.

Fast-forward three years (weekends, evenings, and all) and over 10 different attempts, and . . . ta-da!

1TAM – 1 Thing about Me – Download the app, and let me know what you think.

Post # 37

Banned!

#Thisiswhatticklesme

This will tickle you. Imagine, just imagine . . . you can't catch up on e-mails, you can't check who liked your last 'personal branding' video on LinkedIn, you can't create another group to organise this weekend's plans on WhatsApp, you can't see what your gossipy sister-in-law posted about her vacation on Facebook, and you can't see what your fancy friends had for dinner last night, on Instagram.

Just imagine! You can't do any of these things because your boss just introduced a ban on laptops, tablets, and phones during meetings.

Just people, pens, and notepads (doodling and daydreaming allowed). God forbid, you may end up with:

1. Shorter meetings – you might even be able to cut them and the corporate jargon in half.
2. More focus and better decisions – because there are no distractions or interruptions.

3. Fewer meetings – people will think twice before calling half the company to a meeting, if it means they will be unplugged!

Are you for tech-free meetings?

(Of course, unless you are taking notes on your laptop.)

Post # 38

Five frogs on a log, three decided to jump off. How many left?

#Thisiswhatticklesme

'Mañana', 'tomorrow, Insha Allah' – you know you are in a ticklish situation when you hear those words. I've heard them before too many times, but I haven't gotten used to them. I just repeat them to the sender and add 'NO and NOW' . . .

Not Mañana, NOW (please)!

Agreeing and deciding to do something and talking about doing something are different than actually doing it.

I loved this frog analogy slide when I saw it at a recent conference. It reminded me of a person who has 'decido-phobia' . . . (not difficult to know what phobia that is) – he sits on things for weeks, talks about them, analyses them to boredom, but never gets around to doing anything – it tickles me.

I am sure you know a friend or a colleague who is a Mañana person.

Now I know why I like Nike's famous slogan.

How many frogs are left on the log?

Post # 39

Are chimpanzees smarter than people?

#Thisiswhatticklesme

In 2016, 40 million commercial flights landed safely, and only 10 had fatal accidents. That's 0.000025 per cent.

I like numbers and facts, and I dislike assumptions and speculations. I remember someone telling me 'When you "AssUme", you make an "Ass out of U and Me".'

I am currently devouring this 'fact full' book called *Factfullness*, by Hans Rosling . . . it was written, as the author says, 'To measure ignorance systematically'.

Here are two questions for you:

1. In the last 20 years, the proportion of the world population in extreme poverty has
   A. Almost doubled
   B. Remained more or less the same
   C. Almost halved

2. There are two billion children in the world today, aged between 0 and 15 years of age. How many children will there be in the year 2100?
   A. 4 billion
   B. 3 billion
   C. 2 billion

The book has hundreds of questions and fact-based answers.

What tickled me was that the author found that when tested, the chimpanzees got 33 per cent of the questions right vs humans, who got only 16.6 per cent right.

So! How much do we actually know vs what we think we know?

Post # 40

Let me test your soul!

Thisiswhatticklesme

I have a fastidious friend who always asks philosophical and tickling questions . . . some are pretty silly, but some are thought-provoking.

I know he's about to ask one of those questions when he says, 'Let me test your soul!'

Yesterday he asked me, 'You just won US$10,000. You have only two options:

Option 1: Give the money in full to a children's charity fund. This money will feed, dress, and educate ten kids for a year.

Or

Option 2: Go on a ten-day vacation for two in a super-luxury resort with a personal butler, daily massages, and yoga classes and a life coach.

No third option.

Which option would you go for?'

My first spontaneous and humorous question was, 'Is the mini bar included at the resort?'

I then gave him my unequivocal choice, and we discussed both options for the rest of the evening (I won't bias you with my choice here).

Which option would you go for?

Option 1 or Option 2?

PS. They offer Swedish, aromatherapy, and hot stone massages at the resort.

Post # 41

Women speak 13,000 more words than men per day!

#Thisiswhatticklesme

'She doesn't stop talking!!!' I am sure we've heard that one before. Well, that's because women have higher levels of 'Foxp2 protein' (language protein) – Google it.

It has been claimed that women speak about 20,000 words a day – some 13,000 more than the average man . . .

But not on earnings calls!

A *Bloomberg* article, which tickled me, said (paraphrasing):

> A study of more than 155,000 company conference calls over the past 19 years found that male analysts spoke 92 per cent of the time . . .
>
> Male executives gave more verbose answers to analyst questions than their

> female counterparts . . . because they simply like to hear themselves speak.

(There are more men than women in analyst jobs) Boys! What's going on?

And it really tickled me when I read (according to research):

> 'Female analysts issue bolder and more accurate forecasts and Wall Street knows it.'

My conclusion: I would much rather have more accurate forecasts, to deliver better results, any day vs having to listen to some dude who likes to hear himself talk . . .

It's just good business! I say **#listentoher**

What do you say?

PS. Looking for a female financial advisor.

Post # 42

Are you a boring presenter?

#Thisiswhatticklesme

I almost fell asleep at a recent presentation . . .

Most of us have had a chance or were forced, to stand in front of a crowd and present something.

I know public speaking can be frightening and stressful for some, but we all know how important it is for our careers.

Over the years, I have seen some pretty awesome and some boring presenters.

Good presenters can even make boring topics exciting, and it comes down to three important things:

1. Relevance – know who is in the room!
2. Storytelling – a grabbing intro, a suspense-filled middle, and a convincing end (anecdotes also count).

3. Entertaining – (I am *not* suggesting singing or dancing here) presence, confidence, and some humour.

Three questions your presentation needs to answer (especially to senior executives):

1. What do you want from me, and what's in it for me?
2. What would happen if we don't do this?
3. What is your recommendation and why?

Three things presenters do that tickle me:

1. Read from their slides (I can read, thank you).
2. Ramble on and can't read the audience (even when half of them are fast asleep).
3. Are not prepared (peekaboo, we can see you).

From 1 to 10, how frightened are you of public speaking?

1 = Ready for showbiz.

10 = OMG, I'd rather eat a live scorpion!

Post # 43

Rejection builds character

#Thisiswhatticklesme

We all have been rejected once, twice, many times in our lives! It's humbling, it's tough, it's depressing . . .

I have an old wise friend who always says, 'Get back on your feet, raise your head high, rejection builds character.'

So many successful people had been rejected before they made it.

- Starbucks' Howard Schultz was rejected 242 times by banks.
- J. K. Rowling was rejected 12 times by publishers and for years before Harry Potter was first published.
- Walt Disney's idea of Disneyland was rejected 302 times.

I've been rejected many times too, but I found that every time I got rejected, I learnt something new, and I became more determined, with a sprinkle of grit.

Khaled M. Ismail

It tickles me when I see people crumble and declare defeat – 'I give up,' 'Nobody likes me,' 'I hate my life' – after their first real rejection.

How do you deal with rejection?

Post # 44

Taking your bra off after wearing it for hours – awesome

#Thisiswhatticklesme

I rarely read books cover to cover, and I am not sure I ever will. I am too impatient; I read the intro, scan through the chapters, and maybe read the last two chapters word for word!

Voila! Until I got this *awesome* book by Neil Pasricha . . . thanks, sis.

It made me smile; it made me think . . . that awesomeness is all around us . . . little things are important to happiness.

1. 'The smell of rain on a hot sidewalk'
2. 'Popping bubble wrap'
3. 'Waking up and realising it's Saturday'
4. 'Picking the perfect nacho off someone else's plate'

5. 'Moving clothes from the washer to the dryer without dropping anything'
6. 'Taking your bra off after wearing it for hours . . . it just feels like freedom' . . . or so I've heard.

+ many awesome 'little things' in the book. It tickled me when someone, who shall remain nameless, suggested that I write a book with all my 'what tickles me' posts!

I never thought of myself as an author.

Hmm!

(Confession: I didn't read the above-mentioned book cover to cover either, but it's still awesome.)

Post # 45

Cars are parked 95 per cent of the time!

#Thisiswhatticklesme

'Cars are passé; they are like the fax machine,' said my hardcore environmentalist friend when he came to pick me up to stay at his place during a recent trip to Europe.

'I don't have one because I think they are a waste of space, bad for the environment, and cost a lot of money:

- Cost of the car – when it is parked 95 per cent of the time!
- Insurance and maintenance
- Running cost (petrol in Europe – ouch!)
- Parking costs (in major cities) where a single parking space (5 × 2.5 m) in Hong Kong sold for US$760,000

When I need one, I either take an Uber or I rent this little cute car which uses a small space to park,' he added.

I said, 'I agree with you . . . can we please go? We can discuss this at home . . . I am thirsty for some *organic wine*.'

What tickled me was that he had to order an Uber to take me and my luggage home, because my luggage wouldn't fit in his cute little rent-a-car.

Would you give up your car yet?

Post # 46

Leave them wanting more!

#Thisiswhatticklesme

During a recent 13-hour flight, I had the pleasure of having 'Too Much Information Andy' sitting next to me – yes, I gave him a nickname.

I learned that Andy likes sushi but not 'the raw fish part'; his brother is training for a marathon; his mother gives him a hard time about the fact that he still lives with her; he likes his job, but his boss sucks; and I also learned that his shoe size is 44 – hard to find that size on sale.

Don't get me wrong; I liked Andy, but there was nothing more I wanted to learn about him after five hours into the flight.

Andy didn't practice the 'Leave Them Wanting More' method.

It applies in relationships (maintaining a little mystery), in food (I hate buffets), and in business.

In business, we don't edit enough. For example, a slide with a list of three top priorities invariably includes an 'a, b, and c' below each one – which really means a list of nine, followed by a plethora of slides explaining each priority.

If you are presenting, please don't bore them with granular details, and don't kill them with too much information.

Just enough to get them genuinely interested, and they will ask for more. In short, 'Less Is More'.

How many Andys do you know? (PS. Andy is a fictitious name.)

Post # 47

If you don't respect yourself, no one else will

#Thisiswhatticklesme

After a casual dinner, I was walking home with my son. We found this sign on the side of the road. I paused and read it out loud: 'Will take verbal abuse for spare change.'

I wondered who left it behind!

I thought that was a brilliant, creative, and an eye-catching line to get people's attention and, more importantly, to give the holder money.

It was a bit late for me to try it, and I wasn't sure I would withstand the abuse without abusing them back.

What tickled me was what my son said as we walked on!

'Isn't that what happens in real life at work? You get flak from your boss or a customer; you accept it . . . and keep your job and get paid.'

I said, 'Absolutely *not*!'

If that is the case, it means one of three things:

1. You're working for the wrong company/boss – run.
2. You're really rubbish at 'that' job – find another.
3. If you don't respect yourself, no one else will.

What would you have said to him?

Post # 48

Which letter is silent in the word 'Scent', the S or the C?

#Thisiswhatticklesme

On a warm, cloudless summer vacation day, breathing fresh air, sitting and contemplating things (many things – family, work, whether to have another glass of wine or not) . . .

a couple of thoughts crossed my mind, and some actually tickled me, because I didn't have an answer.

Top Five:

1. Maybe oxygen is slowly killing us, and it just takes 75–100 years to fully work . . .
2. Which letter is silent in the word 'Scent', the *S* or the *C*?
3. Do twins ever realise that one of them is unplanned?
4. How come you never see a headline 'Psychic Wins Lottery'?
5. How would I know that @fitlinda had a kale salad for lunch if we didn't have Instagram?

Bonus: Is it time to go back to work?

What do you question?

Post # 49

You sent 4,000 messages last year

#Thisiswhatticklesme

I have a friend who only sends (and receives) text messages. I wouldn't know what he sounds like on the phone, even if he called me!

We've known each other for over four years, and we only text each other – no calls.

When I call him, he doesn't pick up . . . a couple of minutes later, he sends me a text message.

What's with our obsession with text messages?

28.2 trillion messages were sent from mobile phones in 2017.

That's 4,000 messages per person on this planet per year!

Most people prefer texting vs calling or even e-mailing (for the same message).

What tickles me is that I remember the days when it took me ages attempting to type a short text message on my Nokia, before predictive text became available.

It would be summer before I finished my message of: 'Bring a warm jacket; it's freezing outside!'

Are you a text or a phone person?

Post # 50

Divorced faucets . . . why?

#Thisiswhatticklesme

It was a lovely restaurant with a view. I had a long French/Italian-style lunch that goes on for hours, with a couple of friends. We talked about business, politics, and even touched on logic and common sense.

I ate fries with my fingers, I made a mess, I dropped sauce on my shorts – that was annoying, but the afternoon was splendid.

Until I went to the washroom to wash my hands . . .

I was tickled because I walked out with one blue hand and one red, and probably wasted a Niagara Falls worth of water, as well as bobbled a little.

I asked the restaurant manager, 'Why . . . why . . . the two divorced faucets?'

He suppressed a giggle and said, 'We like to be different!'

Khaled M. Ismail

I've been to England, and I've always wondered why they *still* have two faucets (Cold and Hot) next to each other . . . I do not understand the reason or logic.

Can someone tell me, please?

Post # 51

Your money. Your way. Imagine that!

#Thisiswhatticklesme

I was walking in the big busy city (Toronto) on a pleasant Canadian summer evening, thinking about life and wondering what all the people around me were thinking, where they were going, and what they would have for dinner . . .

Until I saw this sign on top of the entrance of a reputed bank . . . and I got a tiny bit tickled.

Your money. Your way. Imagine that!

Really! Is that the bank's motto? Is that the bank's promise to its customers?

It certainly didn't look like a temporary promotional tagline.

Yes, if it was my money (even if I borrowed it from you), I would surely spend it my way . . . *imagine that*. I would love to know what the bank's CMO was thinking when he/she approved this tagline.

My top three favourite taglines:

- Disney – the happiest place on Earth
- US Postal Service – we deliver
- DeBeers – a diamond is forever

What's your favourite tagline?

Post # 52

Hi, kefak, ça va?

#Thisiswhatticklesme

I was recently 'judged' for speaking a sentence with a hybrid of . . . English, Arabic, and French (a.k.a. Lebanese)

'Hi, kefak, ça va?' (Translation: Hi, how are you, OK?)

A native language is part of any country's identity and culture . . . but one language always creeps in, unless you live in a soundproof bunker.

English! The world's unofficial lingua franca.

No language in history has dominated the world quite like English does today . . . the language of trade, business, finance, diplomacy, science, and the Internet.

Protesting it feels like yelling at the wall!

What tickles me is that every day English spreads, the world becomes a little more homogeneous and a little more bland.

Khaled M. Ismail

And we don't like bland . . . do we?

Thankfully, no matter how global we become, we still have a diversity of cultures, music, art, and food . . . like fish and chips, and mushy peas, tabbouleh, baguette, curry, and dim sum . . . nothing bland about that!

How many cultures do you speak?

Post # 53

My life is captured in photos

#Thisiswhatticklesme

The 'Photos' tab on my phone didn't work this morning. I tried several times, but it didn't open. I had to restart my phone to get it to open. I didn't realise how important that photo gallery was until I was desperate to open it to give a reservation number, which I'd taken a screen shot of. Like many of you, I use the gallery for:

1. Family photos, kids' graduation, special occasions, and silly photos
2. Photos of friends and colleagues (mostly happy moments)
3. Photos of interesting places I visit or things I see
4. Photos of the occasional burger
5. Funny jokes saved from WhatsApp
6. Boarding passes (screen shot of the bar code for easy access)

7. Invoices and receipts (so I can flash it at the snarky store clerk, in case I want to return an item)
8. etc., etc. . . .

What tickles me is that we are so dependent on technology . . . my whole life is captured in photos. In fact, I have 4,620 digital photos and screen shots on my phone. That equates to approximately 80 bulky old-fashioned albums, which could easily fill up half a room!

Which made me think!

Do I have a backup? Now I do! Do you?

How many photos do you have on your phone?

Post # 54

I suffer from 'SFS'!

#Thisiswhatticklesme

Yes, I sometimes suffer from *SFS. Some days are better than others, but when my SFS is high, I tend to get tickled easily.

Here are the top 10 things that tickle me:

1. Speaking in jargon: 'I'll circle back for a high-level convergence meeting to discuss adjacencies.' Who speaks like that?
2. When someone is late for a meeting.
3. When people lie.
4. 'Reply all' to e-mails, when you really don't need to.
5. When people try to get into an elevator before you even have a chance to exit.
6. People who talk or check their bright-lit phones in a movie theatre.
7. When an entitled passenger fully reclines their economy seat on a plane throughout the flight.

8. Finding several spelling mistakes in one e-mail or document.
9. When people overpromise and underdeliver.

And

10. Out-of-office replies like this one: 'I am on vacation for the next four weeks enjoying the sunshine . . . will reply to your e-mail when I am back.' (Actual OOO reply).

What tickles you?

*SFS = Short Fuse Syndrome

Post # 55

Riding a bike without a helmet, remember?

#Thisiswhatticklesme

'Is that an elevator? Look it has no doors . . . that is so cool . . . but also scary and dangerous,' I overheard a woman say when I was checking in at a hotel in Frankfurt last week . . . I found out that it is called a 'Paternoster', and every department store in Germany used to have a paternoster in the late 1960s.

You 'hop on' and 'hop off' when you've reached your desired floor.

And if you are bored, you can stay on the paternoster all day going up and down, because the box you are standing in just keeps going up or down and around again, like a ferris wheel.

What tickles me is the level of paranoia and the safety-conscious world we now live in vs the recent past when:

1. It was OK (legal) to ride a bicycle or ski without a helmet.
2. You drove a car without seat belts.
3. We drank two to three sodas per day.
4. We smoked on airplanes.
5. You climbed trees or walls without a sophisticated safety harness.
6. You had a trampoline in the backyard without a 'three-meter' high net.
7. We hitchhiked.
8. I slept in the back window of the car on road trips.

And

9. Of course, we used elevators without doors!

Sure, we learn, develop, and evolve . . . but can you relate?

What do we do today that will be thought of as 'Wow, unsafe, crazy' in 25–30 years?

Post # 56

Why can't we just print more money?

#Thisiswhatticklesme

I was at my friend's house for dinner when little Mo (age seven) came asking for money to order pizza.

I took US$10 and gave it to him. He said he needed US$15. I said, 'I only have US$10.'

'Why can't you just print more money at the office?' Mo asked. His question tickled me. So, I thought, 'Here is my opportunity to teach seven-year-old Mo how money works.'

I asked him to sit down next to me on the couch. I said, 'Imagine this pile of chocolates in front of us is *all* the food the world can produce per year.'

He gazed at me in horror *'Really?'* he said.

I said, 'Mo, just imagine. If we printed double or triple the amount of money and gave it to people, the *demand* for chocolates will increase, because people can now afford it. But the *supply* of chocolate is limited, so the price of chocolate will double, if not triple (Economics 101) – we call that "inflation".

Then, because everyone has money, there is a high probability that we will run out of chocolate, and we won't be able to use the money to buy anything.

So that's why we can't simply just print money and give it to everyone; otherwise, we could've done that and solved the world's poverty problems.'

Mo looked at me in a daze and said, 'I am going to play Fortnite now.'

He grabbed a handful of chocolates (before they could run out) and ran upstairs.

Post # 57

Can I borrow US$1,700?

#Thisiswhatticklesme

Joe (age 29) and I had a very interesting discussion last night. He was talking about his yoga retreat in Bali and his last trip to Vietnam and his plans for this summer to Ibiza and Madrid.

'Wow, Joe, you must be making loads of money to afford all these trips!' I said.

He got all serious and said, 'I care more about the experiences!'

It got me thinking, so I did some research and found that 72 per cent of today's young adults prefer to spend more money on experiences than on material things, and the top three reasons why are:

1. Experiences define your purpose and passions.
2. Experiences introduce you to a whole new world.
3. Experiences teach you life lessons.

'Love it', I thought, 'I can subscribe to that . . . but at what cost?' The research continued . . .

A 2017 GoBankingRates survey found that most young millennials had less than US$1,000 in their savings accounts, and nearly half had nothing saved at all. Also, the share of these experience-seeking dudes with US$0 in savings is on the rise – 31 per cent in '16 and 46 per cent in '17.

It tickled me when Joe leaned over at the end of the evening and said, 'Can I borrow US$1,700 – until the end of the month – to pay for my car insurance?'

I smirked, paid for dinner, and mumbled, 'Experiences don't pay the bills.'

What am I missing?

Post # 58

Hey, Siri, how great am I?

#Thisiswhatticklesme

'Hey, Siri, am I smart?' I asked.

Siri responded, 'It depends' . . .

Hmm, I thought she would've had a more encouraging answer than that.

Thankfully, she didn't insult me with 'I think you are a 3 out 10'; that would have tickled my day. Then again, she has the right to say whatever her little chip desires. (Bots don't have hearts.)

My phone knows so much about me – who I text and talk to, what I say, the intelligent things I write, where I browse, and what I view.

So, with all the 'AI' powers emerging in the world today, especially with Apple, I thought Siri would be blown away with me! Sadly, that didn't happen.

Khaled M. Ismail

It reminded me of a friend who used to doze off through classes in school – he would always get away with it. Every time a teacher asked him a question, his response would be 'It depends' – so maybe Siri borrowed that line from my friend.

I digress . . . My question is this: Should robots (with super AI capabilities) have the same freedom of speech as we do, with its consequences (where applicable), or should they be exempted?

The tickling question, I know, but one we will have to face sometime soon.

Post # 59

How did we block people in the '80s?

#Thisiswhatticklesme

Someone has been tickling me on LinkedIn for a while. He was practicing pressure sales on me. I said no thanks and politely declined the first time, but he tried again . . .

I said, 'No, thank you' and told him that I will contact him if I ever need his services.

He sent his company profile just in case; I ignored it.

He sent another message telling me that he was wondering why I couldn't see value in his service. I ignored him.

He sent a message accusing me of not responding to his messages.

I blocked him! It tickled me when he sent another promotional message on WhatsApp (he did his homework and found my number).

Khaled M. Ismail

I blocked him!

I reflected on how we used to block sales calls in ancient times when we kept the phone off the hook – it brought back memories.

I smiled.

Post # 60

Culture eats strategy for breakfast

—Peter Drucker

#Thisiswhatticklesme

'What happened to Mark? He just joined three months ago,' I asked my friend Sam last week.

He said, 'Sadly he didn't "fit in" the company culture, so we had to go our separate ways.'

I know Mark – his maturity, capability, and strategic thinking – a solid professional . . . so I was puzzled . . . what went wrong?

From my experience, 'company culture' is implied . . . not expressly defined or written anywhere . . . because it is made up of values, beliefs, and behaviours of how a company's employees and management interact.

I have experienced several types throughout my career, the 'American', the 'Asian', the 'Middle Eastern', the

'European', and the 'Swedish' . . . and some are miles apart.

So, I know the importance of company culture, but can it really dictate who stays and who goes?

What tickled me was that when I spoke to Mark today, he told me that he left his last job because he was told that 'he was too inquisitive, liked to ask "why", and that he questioned authority'.

I am sure you've heard the saying 'Culture eats strategy for breakfast', by Peter Drucker.

So, which do you believe in?

1. People either fit in or they don't.
2. If people try hard, they can fit into any company culture.
3. People should change who they are to fit into a company culture.

Post # 61

No more Mr. Nice Guy . . .

#Thisiswhatticklesme

'That's it, I've had it,' said exasperated *Roy. 'This is the second time I get passed up for a promotion to an $and@$ . . . that's it, *no more Mr. Nice Guy*,' he added.

The feedback he got was that his leadership style was not firm enough to drive a team and not hungry enough to convince his customers – to be the next sales director.

'You are too nice!' he was told.

I reflected . . .

Do I prefer 'nice guys' who work super hard and create a collaborative and good working environment at work, or 'shrewd, tickling hustlers' . . . who will not take *no* for an answer, do anything to get the job done or make the next sale . . . and create a competitive environment?

I then remembered what an old man once told me at the beginning of my career:

> A nice guy can marry my daughter . . . but not run my business.

Now over to you!

Who would you want on your team/to drive your business – 'a nice guy/gal' or a 'ruthless hustler'?

Disclaimer: *'Roy' is a fictitious name . . . No Roy I know has been passed up for a promotion in real life nor hurt in the making of this post.

Post # 62

I am CrеAtIvе!

#Thisiswhatticklesme

Everyone who's everyone is now talking, writing, and posting about personal branding and how important it is for career success.

I fully agree with the idea that each of us is a walking and living brand which needs to be nurtured, managed, and promoted . . . without overdoing it!

Some brand ambassadors and preachers are awesome and actually walk the talk! Not sure about the credentials and credibility of others.

SPECIAL OFFER

If you were offered a free billboard on Main Street for one week to *promote* your *brand* and what you stand for, what three words or sentences would you put on it that best describes you?

Khaled M. Ismail

My three words:

- Pragmatic
- Resilient
- Creative

Post # 63

Are you as finicky as I am?

#Thisiswhatticklesme

Is it just me? I noticed that the 'older' I get, the finickier I get in certain situations . . . I used to have more patience, but now I don't.

Is it just me, or do you know right away when:

1. Someone is trying to sell you pink flying elephants (lie)
2. Someone is giving you the 'attitude'
3. You'd rather watch paint dry than stand in a queue to get into a restaurant or club
4. You'd much rather knit a sweater than listen to a boring presentation that's full of jargon
5. You'd rather just walk away than argue with a friend about why the chicken crossed the road or whether the size of your head affects your IQ

And the one that tickles me . . .

    6.   You'd rather have acupuncture done on your face than listen to someone who constantly whines

Maybe it is just me!

Post # 64

Humans only use 10 per cent of the brain's capacity. What???

#Thisiswhatticklesme

I like smart people, sharp people, people who think before they open their mouths, people who are eloquent and can clearly articulate what they want you to know or do.

I find it stimulating and at times even appealing.

I am sure you've heard the saying or myth that humans only use 10 per cent of the brain's capacity. Imagine if we could use 100 per cent of our brain . . .

Wow . . . wouldn't that be swell?

I've struggled with that notion because I can't accept that I am only using 10 per cent. Surely I can use more . . . but how? What should I do?

After some research, I learnt that to increase the utilisation of my brain, I have to:

1. Exercise – yup, sometimes
2. Drink coffee – I do that daily
3. Sleep well – ditto
4. Eat well – ditto, sometimes too much
5. Get some sunlight – I live in Dubai
6. Read – I read too many e-mails daily
7. Play Tetris – I have my good days

Today I woke up determined to use at least 15 per cent of my brain, squeeze out another 5 per cent. What tickled me was that I couldn't come up with any new revelations . . . and I ended up making a mighty omelette, coffee, and writing this blog (check pts 2 and 4 above).

What do you do to stimulate your brain for maximum utilisation?

Post # 65

Diamond bracelet or car?

#Thisiswhatticklesme

I was feeling a little generous and wanted to buy my daughter a diamond bracelet for her 21st birthday because I was told that 'Diamonds are a girl's best friend.'

I happened to be with my practical and frugal friend Bruce.

'Why are you buying her carbon?' he said. 'Buy her something practical she can use,' he added. 'Did you know that as soon as you leave the jeweller, the diamond loses more than 50 per cent of its value, and with the same money you can buy her a second-hand car?'

After extensive research (10 min on Google) I found that not only is the demand for diamonds a marketing invention (including the tagline 'Diamonds are forever'), but diamonds aren't actually that rare in comparison to other gemstones. Only by restricting supply have *big* suppliers kept the price of diamonds high.

Khaled M. Ismail

What tickles me is that the value of all my diamonds can now just buy me a venti almond latte with a double shot.

Back to my daughter – diamond bracelet or car?

Post # 66

Don't you know who I am?

#Thisiswhatticklesme

'You are in my seat!' said six-year-old Sarah* to me with authority. I was thinking of responding with 'Don't you know who I am?' But I refrained because I knew Sarah couldn't care less.

Spending time with the kids today at the Parent and Child Wellbeing Conference was an eye-opener.

It was refreshing to see how times have changed; how creative and switched on kids are today vs 20 years ago; and how parents look at parenting, nutrition, and the wellbeing of their (our) children.

One nutrition-savvy parent felt a sense of success when kids at her children's recent birthday party did *not* recognise the names of two *major* multinational fast-food chains.

What tickles me is that if I attempted (15 years ago) to drive past a famous fast-food restaurant with my two kids without stopping on a Saturday evening, I think I would've been disowned or beaten up.

Times, food safety, and nutrition issues have certainly evolved and changed, and I don't expect them to stop anytime soon.

What's important is that my kids still love me (I think), even though I have embarrassed them on numerous occasions, and that they are both healthy.

PS: *'Sarah' is not the snappy six-year-old's real name, and we became friends in the end!

Post # 67

Sushi tikka masala!

#Thisiswhatticklesme

'Let's go for sushi,' I said to my friend Rizwan. At first, he was hesitant, but I managed to convince him. I knew that he would've much preferred to have chicken tikka masala and mutton biryani.

As we were ordering at the restaurant, he whispered, 'I don't like sushi; isn't it raw fish?'

I launched into a sushi history lesson.

Khaled M. Ismail

Sushi began in the rice fields of Southeast Asia, before moving to Japan in the eighth century, where fish was preserved in salt and fermented rice, after which the rice was discarded.

The word 'sushi' doesn't mean 'raw fish'. It actually refers to a rice dish, flavoured with rice vinegar and served with various fillings and toppings, including raw fish. Also, after visiting Japan a couple of times, I was surprised to discover that Japanese people don't actually eat sushi very often!

What tickled me was after an enjoyable dinner for me, and an awkward and excruciating one for Rizwan, which cost us an arm and a leg . . . he grabbed my arm at the door, leaned towards me, and mumbled, 'Challo, yaar, sahi khaana khatey hain!' . . . Meaning 'Come on, dude, let's go eat some proper food!'

I mumbled back, 'We should've ordered some sushi tikka masala!'

If looks could kill!

Post # 68

I am lit, I am hip, I can't even

#Thisiswhatticklesme

We all grew up watching TV commercials; some stuck with us, and some didn't. Remember these taglines?

- Just do it
- Where's the beef?
- Good to the last drop
- Melts in your mouth, not in your hands
- Don't leave home without it

I bet you remember some of them, and you would even know which brands they are for.

Why?

Because these messages were simple, relevant to the brand's USP, and were repeated for years and years.

The key word here is 'repeated'. Marketing experts debate on what is the 'effective frequency' for a message to stick, and for consumers to take notice. Some say repeating a message three times will work, while many believe the 'Rule of 7' applies.

Also, studies suggest that the more you repeat a message, the more truthful it becomes. In short, repeat it, believe it.

That is because presumably repetition imbues familiarity, and familiarity breeds trust.

What tickles me is that no matter how many times I tell my kids that their dad is lit and hip and I repeat that . . . they don't seem to agree with me or believe me.

I repeat,

I am lit, I am hip, I can't even . . .

Do you believe me now?

Post # 69

Newspapers vs Facebook

#Thisiswhatticklesme

'This was a breach of trust and I'm sorry we didn't do more at the time,' writes Zuckerberg. 'I promise to do better for you.'

Facebook on Sunday took out full-page ads in seven British newspapers and three American ones to apologise for the ongoing Cambridge Analytica data privacy scandal involving the social network in a legal and regulatory nightmare.

I, Khaled, accept his apology because I don't think its Facebook's fault. I signed up on Facebook knowing full well that my data will be used, just like on any social platform . . . someone else messed up. Moving on . . .

What tickles me though is that to legitimise his apology, he had to do it the old-fashioned way . . . using *newspapers*!

Think about it: He could have sent his message directly to millions of people to their bedside tables in the morning (where we all keep our phones overnight), for *free*, but he chose to pay for full-page newspaper ads!

Do you see the irony?

Post # 70

Please don't 'circle back'!

#Thisiswhatticklesme

Today I received an e-mail from someone who was 'circling back' with me on a message (sales pitch) they sent me a week ago.

I cringed!

We all have words that 'ruffle our feathers'. For me, the words that tickle me are

'Be authentic'
'Reaching out' and
'Circling back' . . .

Please don't!

Why can't you just
'Be yourself'
'Contact/call me' and
'Get back to me' instead!

Please 'circle back', and tell me which word(s) you dislike.

Post # 71

I think you have Athazagoraphobia

#Thisiswhatticklesme

We all have a fear of something. Most fears are learnt . . . spiders, heights, the dark – these are called natural fears, usually developed at a young age or influenced by experiences, our environment, and culture.

The usual and common ones:

- Acrophobia – fear of heights
- Pteromerhanophobia – fear of flying
- Claustrophobia – fear of enclosed spaces
- Glossophobia – fear of public speaking
- Atychiphobia – fear of failure

The unusual ones:

- Chrometophobia – fear of money (I can solve that one for you)

#Thisiswhatticklesme

- Athazagoraphobia – fear of being forgotten or ignored (Come on, admit it)
- Syngenesophobia – fear of relatives (I can relate)
- Nomophobia – fear of being without mobile phone coverage

And the one that tickles me

- Hippopotomonstrosesquippedaliophobia – fear of long words . . .

I would be afraid if I saw a word that long.

A tickling question: Why do we have to learn Greek to understand these unpronounceable phobias?

Why can't we just call them by what they are?

No one says, 'He has Hexakosioihexekontahexaphobia.'

We say, 'He has a fear of the # 666.'

What is your biggest fear?

Post # 72

I am thrilled . . . I can't even

#Thisiswhatticklesme

I thought I spoke English . . . until . . . I was sitting next to my son as he was chatting online with a couple of friends – and he let me peep in . . .

I noticed that I had to ask him several times to explain what that word or letters meant.

These guys have developed their own Internet 'slang' language, which I pretend to understand . . . but I realised that I am actually #illiterate

Here are the top 10 of what I learnt:

1. IMHO = In my humble opinion
2. IRL = In real life
3. IDC = I don't care
4. Totes = Totally
5. Lit = When something is amazing

6. Pwned = Intentional misspelling of the word 'owned'. Meaning someone got defeated or humiliated
7. ELI5 = Explain like I'm five years old
8. GOAT = Greatest of all time
9. JSYK = Just so you know

And the one that tickles me is

10. 'I Can't Even' – slang expression used to indicate speechlessness, from overjoy or exasperation

So, let me ELY5 – IMHO, I am totes the Goat when it comes to Internet slang. JSYK, I am feeling Lit today and IDC if I get pwned.

'I Can't Even'!

Do you speak internet?

Post # 73

Flip-flops to work?

#Thisiswhatticklesme

Temperatures are slowly rising, and the layers are coming off, revealing more skin. Early in my career, I was told, 'You look more professional when you're well dressed,' 'They'll take you more seriously,' or 'Dress like you want your manager's/boss's job.'

So, I concluded that what you wear at work is important!

According to research, appearance ranked second only to communication skills when respondents named qualities most often associated with professionalism.

Business attire has changed significantly over the years, especially in the last 20 years – smart casual is *'in'*, even for some CEOs, allowing employees to dress the way that suits their personality and comfort.

I was recently at a cool and trendy dentist's office, and one associate looked like she was going to the beach.

#Thisiswhatticklesme

Fancy flip-flops and all (I will spare you the details – use your imagination).

It tickled me. I thought, 'That's super casual!' I found it a bit OTT.

Noted, some industries are different than others – like 'creatives and geeks', but they both face 'The Customer'.

How would you feel if your banker or lawyer showed up with ripped jeans and sandals?

Post # 74

Do you need a one-hour-long hug? (70 calories)

#Thisiswhatticklesme

For years I've wanted to have a 'six pack', you know, the type that looks like it's been sculpted on your stomach! Not the 'six can' type.

Every weekend I attempt to do some serious exercise with the hope that my six pack decides to come out of hiding – I know it's there, it's just a bit shy.

My weekend exercise routine consists of swimming, walking, volleyball, cycling – the low-impact type, with an objective to burn about 1,000 calories per day.

I was tickled this morning when I read an article that spelled out how we can burn calories without the agonising effort of exercise:

1. Brushing your teeth for 3 min burns 10 calories.
2. Dancing for 10 min burns 50 calories.

#Thisiswhatticklesme

3. Singing in the shower can burn 10–20 calories per song.
4. Laughing for 10 min can burn 30–40 calories.
5. Hugging for 1 hour can burn 70 calories.
6. Constant texting can burn 40 calories per hour.
7. Banging your head against the wall burns 150 calories per hour.

Looking at these, I doubt my ambition of a 'six pack' will come true anytime soon.

What do you do to burn the most calories?

Post # 75

How creative are you?

#Thisiswhatticklesme

We met the 'other' Mark today at the Marketing Society event at Facebook's offices in Dubai. Mark D'Arcy – chief creative officer – who started his career as a copywriter in New Zealand. I didn't know they had copywriters in New Zealand.

Yes, we only focused on creativity (this is Mark's cup of tea) and its importance in our marketing and communications world!

What my brain picked up from that early-morning session, which was moderated by Asad ur Rehman, was:

- Creativity is not exotic, it is a practical process – you've got to learn it.
- Everyone is a 'creative' now! Look at what people are posting online – even 14-year-old Lucy, whose post went viral!

- There are three pillars to creativity:

    1. Curiosity (obvious!)
    2. Generosity (be willing to exchange, give and take ideas)
    3. Accountability (be responsible towards what you put out there)

What tickles me is now I have to look at each ad as 'an uninvited dinner guest' because, according to Mark, it needs to earn its place at the 'table'!

I have had so many uninvited, tickling, and unwanted guests at my dinner table . . .

Haven't you?

Post # 76

From 1 to 10, how happy are you?

#Thisiswhatticklesme

This will tickle you. I recently noticed, on and off LinkedIn, that there are many unhappy, unemployed people desperately looking for a job; then there are those with a job who are unhappy with it and are looking for another or are hoping to work less.

Hmm! Let's dissect this one.

We all want and desire to be working and happy, but . . .

Being unemployed is tough, discouraging; you tend to get distant, disengaged, ask questions you don't have answers to, blame others . . . all this impacts your attitude and how you're perceived in job interviews.

Not a pretty picture!

On the other hand, many of those with a job say that their work is the primary source of their dissatisfaction. They are not happy; they complain about work/life balance and buy bestselling books that claim to have the answers for how they can work less and be happier.

All of the above tickles me.

My conclusion: If you have a job which earns you a living, be happy and be grateful . . . and let's hope it is a job you love.

And if you don't have a job, 'get it together', *hustle* – don't expect it to land in your lap, and all the power to you in finding a job you love.

I wish you all a pleasant 'International Day of Happiness' – 20 March.

Post # 77

Blood type A – Pragmatists
Conservative, Responsible, Cautious, Punctual

Blood type B – Adventurers
Unpredictable, Passionate, Confident, Impulsive

Blood type AB – Thinkers
Understanding, Organized, Rational, Cool

Blood type O – Leaders
Natural Leaders, Ambitious, Confident, Sociable

#Thisiswhatticklesme

After a few minutes of pleasantries, the first question I was asked by a Japanese acquaintance I met in a restaurant yesterday was, 'What's your blood type?'

Huh!

I was tickled and thought, 'It's none of his business,' 'How weird,' and 'Why would he ask me this "personal" question?'

#Thisiswhatticklesme

But then I quickly learnt that Haruki came in peace and had no ninja-like intentions for me.

I also learnt that the Japanese, along with other Asian cultures, believe that blood type says something about your personality and indicates your compatibility with friends.

'Oh wow!' I said to Haruki in astonishment.

He asked in confirmation, 'Your blood type is O?'

I said, 'How did you know?'

He said, 'You just told me!'

Haruki and I were apparently compatible, so we hit it off for the rest of the night – I have an O+ blood type and he has A+.

This is similar to how astrological signs are perceived in other cultures . . .

So now we have two scientifically unproven methods of compatibility.

What's your blood type?

Post # 78

He has mental-health issues

#Thisiswhatticklesme

'Sara is having a bad day' or 'Sami woke up on the wrong side of the bed' is what we tend to say when a colleague reacts aggressively to a situation or a question.

The reality is maybe they are going through a 'silent' breakdown.

The truth is that we don't know because no one talks about their mental health. It's scary, it's a taboo, it is a 'career-limiting move'.

A friend of mine recently left his job because of the stress and anxiety he was facing at work.

I was a little surprised, 'Is he that sensitive?' I thought!

#Thisiswhatticklesme

What tickles me is that when we talk about someone who has 'mental-health issues', we tend to box them and some may say, 'S/he belongs in a "looney bin."'

We tend to associate 'physical health' with positive thoughts like 'running', 'gym', 'fit', 'healthy', or 'having the flu'.

But 'mental health' is perceived negatively. And we need to change that.

So, I propose we start with changing the name to 'mental well-being' . . . this surely won't solve the problem, but it's the first step . . . then we talk about it – create awareness.

Who's with me?

Post # 79

I am so important, my job title is . . .

#Thisiswhatticklesme

'I won't speak to anyone below a VP or CEO level,' said a gentleman who was at a business meeting today.

It tickled me . . . I thought, 'Really? How uncool.'

He was full of himself and borderline arrogant . . . but he justified himself by saying, 'I want to speak to someone my level, someone who makes decisions and gets things done.'

He then looked at me inquisitively and said, 'What do you do?'

I paused for a moment . . . and said, 'I am not sure I am at your level, but I do a delicious cappuccino. Would you like one?'

#Thisiswhatticklesme

To some, job titles matter a lot. They speak of their status, expertise, and success.

By the way, some people on LinkedIn have interesting job titles.

How much do job titles matter to you?

Post # 80

Professionals impress me

#Thisiswhatticklesme

'I don't really care what mood you are in and what's going on in your life! Just deliver . . . please' is what the 'customer' is thinking.

That's what 'professionals' have to deal with day in and day out.

It's tough . . . but that's life.

I come across many amazing people every day in the service industry who have to be on 'top of their game', regardless of what is going on in their lives.

What tickles me is Ivan Ostapov (in the picture), who is always smiling, no matter what.

#Thisiswhatticklesme

He impresses me!

That's what professionals do, no matter what business they are in.

Cheers to Ivan and every professional out there – one who delivers a service with a smile – who earn a living, regardless of the circumstances in their life.

Thank someone you appreciate for what they do – as professionals.

Post # 81

Men are from Mars and Women . . . we love them

#Thisiswhatticklesme

We all have a woman in our lives. They are wonderful, even though they can be a pain in the neck sometimes.

What tickles me is men will never be able to understand women, *ever* – because they are from Venus, and we are from Mars.

Regardless, I wouldn't want it any other way. Women are the sunshine of our lives. They are our mothers (we all have one), our wives, our sisters, our colleagues, and our friends.

#Thisiswhatticklesme

Besides my mother and my wife, one special woman in my life is my daughter. She is away from me . . . studying in Canada, and I celebrate her and all the other women in our lives on this special day.

Happy International Women's Day . . . all the power to you.

Post # 82

How thick is your ego?

#Thisiswhatticklesme

I recently attended a business event and met a bunch of talented and interesting people. Like any event, you meet new people, you chitchat, and you exchange business cards.

But this event was different because there were many VIPs with titles like Honorary Mr. X, Her Excellency Ms. Y, and the occasional accomplished Hedge Fund Manager Z.

#Thisiswhatticklesme

What tickled me was the thickness of their business cards. The more important the person, the thicker their business card . . . some even with painted edges.

Tickling and hilarious at the same time!

My question is this: In this digital day and age, why do we still exchange business cards? There's got to be a better, modern, and more environmentally friendly way to introduce yourself and even show off how important you are.

(You know where most of the cards end up after you enter the details into your phone!)

What I now do (sometimes) is scan and return their card! (Awesome app b.t.w.)

Do you still exchange business cards?

PS. I measured it, 4 of my business cards = 1 VIP's card!

Therefore, he was 4× more important than me.

Post # 83

What do happy people do?

#Thisiswhatticklesme

Driving to a dinner event this weekend, I stopped at a traffic light, and I saw this sign. There is a street in Dubai called 'Happiness St'!

I knew that the government recently announced the formation of the Ministry of Happiness with a minister and all.

Hmm! A ministry with a vision, mission, and objectives, and now a street... this is serious, so I decided to investigate.

They have five objectives:

1. Harmonise the government's plans and polices to achieve happiness and positivity in society.

#Thisiswhatticklesme

2. Incentivise entities to launch initiatives, projects, and policies to achieve happiness.
3. Propose strategic policies and programmes to achieve happiness.
4. Instil a culture of happiness and positivity as a lifestyle.
5. Develop KPIs to measure happiness with government's entities.

Genius! I thought.

What tickles me is this: Why aren't enough companies introducing the 'Department of Happiness' with the same objectives?

Fact: Happy people are more productive, more engaged, more creative, take fewer sick days, are better leaders, close more sales . . . no rocket science there.

Don't take my word for it . . . research doesn't lie.

I am happy but a little tickled, aren't you?

Post # 84

Success is a choice

#Thisiswhatticklesme

He is a total nutcase! He speaks with his energy and body language; he is entertaining, funny, and thought provoking.

Robin Banks, an international speaker extraordinaire, came to speak at our Tetra Pak annual conference in Dubai today.

'Success is a choice' was the title of his talk.

When I wasn't jumping or laughing, I managed to jot down five takeaways to share with you:

- It is *our* choice how we react to tickling situations.
- *Let go* of crippling and negative thoughts 'luggage' – they hold you back.
- If toddlers gave up on walking after they fell the first time they tried, we'd all be crawling now! Don't give up, ever.

- When you wake up in the morning and decide to have an awesome day . . . there is a high probability that *you will*.
- Positive energy is contagious.

His energy tickled me; I got tired of watching him. He couldn't stand still; half the time he was either on top of a chair or crawling.

Final thought

Success is not an accident; success is actually a choice
—Stephen Curry

Post # 85

Free Valentine's Day cake

#Thisiswhatticklesme

The price of flowers double, restaurants are painted red, the price of chocolate goes up (+VAT) on Valentine's Day, which results in:

- more than 1 billion cards exchanged around the world
- more than 50 million roses given
- more than 36 million heart-shaped boxes of chocolates sold

In the US alone, Valentine's Day contributes more than US$18.5 billion to the economy.

I am not an enthusiastic fan of Valentine's Day. I think it has become too commercial with desperate creativity.

Having said that, who would be tickled if they received 50 roses, a pair of shoes, a box of chocolates, a bottle of champagne . . . oh . . . and a free Valentine's cake?

Would you?

Post # 86

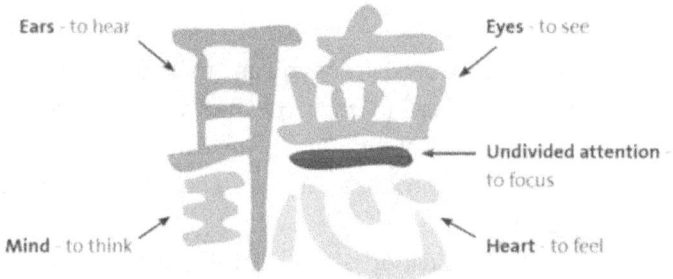

Source: Will Taylor

#Thisiswhatticklesme

How many times did this happen to you: You are talking to a friend or colleague about something super important and you notice that they have 'vacant' eyes! – Not really with you!

'Are you listening to me?' you shout!

To be honest, when we are in a conversation, we're usually thinking of how we will respond or what's for dinner. Very few of us are fully engaged and deeply listening.

We like people who are 'good listeners' because they make us feel that they care.

I didn't know that the Chinese cracked the art and spirit of listening in one symbol meaning 'to listen', which is made up of five characters.

1. Ears – Obviously! What you use to hear information
2. Eyes – Observing as if you had ten eyes (this is also the symbol for 10)
3. Mind – To process, understand, and interpret information
4. Focus – Undivided attention without distraction
5. Heart – Caring and understanding the emotions involved

What tickles me is now I have to rethink my listening skills . . . my wife says I don't listen to her . . . at least I think that's what she said . . .

Post # 87

Gamified obedience!

#Thisiswhatticklesme

Imagine this: 'Harry (650 pts) met Sally (880 pts) at Star Coffee (691 pts).' The # is not their weight, height, or blood pressure . . . this is their social score out of 1,000.

Hmm!

In 2020, China is proposing to introduce a Social Credit System for developing a national reputation system.

It works as a real time mass surveillance tool and uses big data analysis technology from people's everyday activities, online and offline, to regulate the economy and as a tool to steer citizens' behaviour.

Citizens will have to comply with policies and regulations to avoid having their scores lowered.

People and companies with a good score will enjoy benefits such as lower tax rates, faster services, status in society, etc.

Don't blink; a similar system will be introduced near you sooner than you think . . . after all, what will we do with all this big data?

Obedience sounds like a good idea! And gamifying it sounds like fun.

Examples of application:

- If your score is less than 700 pts – don't bother applying for a job here.
- Earn 25 pts if you don't use your car today!
- Harry pays US$1.17 for coffee, and Sally pays US$1.
- Tickling posts like this would lower your score by 10 pts.

Post # 88

Do some research on fancy cars and mega yachts

#Thisiswhatticklesme

Fire sale – bargain basement prices. Or is it? 17 December 2017, Bitcoin hit US$20K. Ever since, it's been descending smoothly like an A380.

I am not sure where it will land, but when it falls it will crash land, before it takes off again.

But I am fairly sure of a couple of things:

- There is a lot of market manipulation and wild speculation, with a heavy dose of 'pump and dump'.
- If you're going to take the plunge into cryptocurrency, be prepared to lose it . . . all of it. (On the other hand, do some research on fancy cars and mega yachts as well.)

- It is insanely attractive to imagine the amount of money you could make in a short period of time (and the opposite is also true).
- Cryptocurrency is here to stay – I have no doubt about it. The question is this: In what form?
- And *when*, not if, banks and governments accept, regulate, and adopt it, it will explode, like the smartphones with no keypad did.

Here is my two bitcoins' worth.

!!Disclaimer!!: This is purely my opinion. So, if you buy and lose, don't blame me . . . and if you buy and make a truckload of money, I am OK with 25 per cent of profit (principal aside).

Post # 89

Where there is falafel, there are habibis

#Thisiswhatticklesme

I didn't realize how important this dish is. They are fighting over it!

I am talking about falafel.

The origin of falafel is unknown and controversial. A common theory is that the dish originated in Egypt a couple of thousand years ago.

Some Middle Eastern countries argue that it is their own; others have filed for copyright infringement against other countries in the name of falafel.

Jordan broke the record in 2012 for making the largest falafel (74.75 kg).

You can find it in the Middle East (of course), in Europe, the Americas, and generally where there are more than two habibis.

Falafel is for everyone, vegetarians and vegans, rich and poor.

I used to buy a Falafel sandwich for less than US$1 . . . and I recently had a falafel sandwich in Dubai for more than US$6.

What tickles me is that no one is suing for copyright infringement or arguing over where sushi or Yorkshire pudding originated from!

Post # 90

Fish, Elephant, Same, Same!

#Thisiswhatticklesme

There is at least one in every office and sometimes amongst family and friends. No one can see it, but everyone feels it.

People play peekaboo with it but are not brave enough to bring it out completely. We all know it's there, but no one talks about it.

Because it is sometimes awkward, confrontational, controversial, sensitive, etc. . . .

It's the 'elephant in the room'!

Some elephants are big, and some are small . . .

And where I work, we call it fish!

When we want to discuss the 'elephant in the room', we say:

'Let's put the fish on the table.'

Meaning: don't leave it under the table, otherwise it will rot and stink.

What tickles me is that we use animals to describe or represent our problems!

Poor animals! If only they knew.

How many times have you put the fish on the table?

Post # 91

Don't worry; we are agile

#Thisiswhatticklesme

Another overused and abused word in the business world. It is part of many companies' values or brand positioning, but some still pay 'lip service' to it.

The word 'agile'!!!

It tickles me when a company website says, in big letters, 'We Are Agile', and it took them three weeks to respond to my e-mail requesting a copy of a certificate for something I paid for.

Several times I called to enquire, and I was told, 'Habibi, not to worry', that my request is being processed and that it is with 'the concerned department'.

I blew a gasket and sent a message to their CEO. saying:

'Your company is *not* agile . . . it has many "warm bodies" who don't care, but they must be rewarded for following processes!'

PS. The CEO never responded to my e-mail. To be fair, his assistant called to hear me vent!

What does 'agile' mean to you?

Post # 92

My head is spinning!

#Thisiswhatticklesme

You are in your head! The rest of your body can be replaced, and you will continue to be *you*!

Really?

Science and medicine continue to surprise me! We talk about the speed of change on the technology and communication front, but what's happening, in parallel, in the medical field is mind boggling.

I was amazed to learn that Italian neuroscientist Dr. Sergio Canavero recently (November 2017) performed a successful 'test' head replacement surgery on a corpse, and he will soon perform the same surgery on a live person in China.

Ethical? Moral? Some say, 'Absolutely not!'

Controversial? 'Super'!

Khaled M. Ismail

What tickles me is that there were similar ethical and moral reservations before the first heart transplant, hand transplant, facial transplant transpired.

My head is spinning!!! Excuse the pun.

How do you feel about having your head attached to someone else's body?

Post # 93

What do TVs and textbooks have in common?

#Thisiswhatticklesme

You wonder why it costs an arm and a leg to see a doctor?

There is a theory that anything 'new' commands a premium – for its novelty.

Whenever a product or service is introduced in the market, you expect it to be 'overpriced', and as it becomes more available (with competition

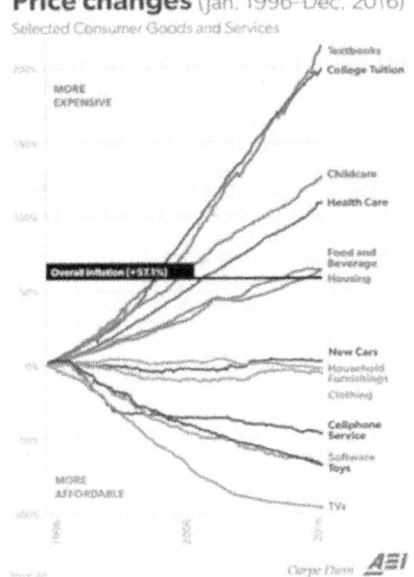

and copycats), the price stabilises or in some cases, decreases over time!

What tickles me is that textbooks and higher education have been around for decades, and their cost continues to skyrocket (~200 per cent over the past 20 years), when the average inflation for the same period was ~57 per cent.

You would've thought that the cost of higher education would go down, especially now that the number of universities in the world have quintupled (5×) since the 1950s to today's ~26K+.

That could be a case of artificially inflating demand for something and not letting supply adjust – prices will go up.

Hmm! (A topic for another post.)

Do you know how much it costs for a student to become a doctor?

Source: Bureau of Labour Statistics.

Post # 94

'I skipped school to do this presentation'

#Thisiswhatticklesme

'Yes, I skipped school to do this presentation,' he said!

How much do you know about e-sports?

One thing is for sure . . . my son (17-year-old semi-professional gamer) knows a ton more than I do about a parallel world that is growing exponentially, which we should take notice of.

Bradley presented at the Marketing Society's Brave Conference in Dubai to 100+ senior marketers about that parallel universe.

Did you know that:

- By 2020, e-sports sponsorship revenue will reach US$2.5 billion?

- In 2016, the Coca-Cola Company sponsored the League of Legends World Championship Series, instead of the Super Bowl?
- An e-sports gamer (player) can earn up to US$1 million per tournament? (This one tickles me a little – I am in the wrong profession.)
- The International Olympic Committee is considering e-sports for future games?

I loved it when he said:

> We're used to not being taken seriously . . .
> If you talk *to* us and not *at* us, we'll be on the same playing field, and it will be way easier for you guys to be involved in our world.

#proud

Post # 95

Buy a luxury home and get a Tesla – guaranteed

#Thisiswhatticklesme

Yesterday evening, I was driving along on my merry way, and I came across this giant billboard!

Buy a luxury home and get a Tesla – guaranteed

I am an environmentalist at heart, and I like the idea of having an electric car.

I called the # on the billboard to enquire about how I can get my Tesla car *guaranteed*!

I asked the salesperson to tell me more about the offer!

What I heard part confused me and part tickled me!

He said, 'When you buy a villa, you get a Tesla guaranteed, but this offer ends soon!'

He continued without me probing, 'But if you don't want the car, we will reduce the price of the villa by Y.'

Y being the cost of the Tesla!

So, I said, 'Let me see if I understood you correctly – you guarantee that I will get the Tesla if I pay for it; otherwise, if I don't want it, you'll deduct the cost of the car from the price of the villa?'

He said, 'Yes that's correct.'

Phew!

I have been in marketing for a silly long time, but I can't put my finger on what type of marketing this is!

There are pull and push marketing strategies; this is neither . . . maybe this is a new one called 'Tickle marketing'.

Please help me.

Post # 96

Would you hire someone with depression or mental-health problems?

#Thisiswhatticklesme

Another buzz word? A taboo subject for sure.

I hear people talk about this topic a lot lately, but do they understand what it *really* means?

Someone recently told me, 'It's great that more people feel able to talk about their mental health.' I found out that there's even a World Mental Health Day (10 October).

Hmm! Just stop for one moment, and look around you!

Every third person you meet (yes one-third of the population) has experienced either depression or mental-health issues.

More than half of the employers would not employ someone with depression/mental-health issues even if they were the best candidate for the job.

Mental health includes emotional, psychological, and social well-being. It affects how we think, feel, handle stress, relate to others, and make choices.

Harassment and bullying at work can have a substantial adverse impact on mental health.

Some early-warning signs:

- Eating or sleeping too much or too little.
- Having little or no energy.
- Feeling helpless or hopeless.
- Feeling unusually confused, forgetful, on edge, angry, worried, or scared.
- Experiencing severe mood swings that cause problems in relationships.

Or is this a new name for good old 'stress'? So . . .

Would you hire someone with depression or mental-health problems?

Post # 97

Are you addicted?

#Thisiswhatticklesme

This weekend . . . I was watching, observing, and taking notes!

I came across many scenes like this! Everyone on the table, everyone in the room, everyone waiting for the bus or train, all were on their smartphones.

New research shows that young adults use their smartphones roughly 2× as much as they estimate that they do.

In fact, the study found that young adults used their phones an average of five hours a day – that's roughly one-third of their total waking hours.
 (Average varies by country.)

Shall we call it what it is?

Does the word 'addiction' come to mind?

What tickles me is that considering it's called a mobile phone, using our mobile device to call people was actually the sixth most used function after activities like checking social media and gaming . . . people don't talk anymore.

I thought, 'What would these young adults do if we took away their smartphones?'

Let's put 'them' aside!

Would *you* give up your phone for a day?

What would you do with all that free time?

Post # 98

Genius Paperboy in Montréal!

#Thisiswhatticklesme

In my teens, I was a paperboy, doing the daily morning route in suburban Montréal, along with my army of paperboys on bicycles.

We used to fling newspapers and sometimes coupons for car washes and chocolate-covered peanuts.

We didn't know what happened after the bundle landed on Linda's doorstep and Sami's porch.

I used to think 'If Sami didn't have a car and Linda had a peanut allergy, what would they do with these coupons?' What a waste.

Fast-forward to 'marketing automation' (MA) of today!

Some may argue that MA is simply 'e-mail marketing' or 'spam'; others wouldn't have a clue to what it means.

MA is a software that enables advertisers to know about who they are e-mailing these coupons to, based on the receivers specific user profile and website patterns.

They would know things like:

- Whether Sami actually has a car
- Whether Sami opened the e-mail with the car wash coupon and clicked on it
- Not to send Linda peanut coupons
- What should be in the subject line to attract Linda's attention
- Whether Sami has a crush on Linda (kidding)

So, MA enables targeted and relevant content, more efficiency, less waste, and analytics, which tells you what to do next time.

It tickles me that a paperboy like me was 'not just smart, but a genius' to think about marketing automation at that age!

Post # 99

Spot the difference: Digitisation vs Digitalisation

#Thisiswhatticklesme

It tickles me that many people still don't know – (some pretend but fail miserably) – the difference between two terms:

Digitisation vs Digitalisation

To be fair, they are linked and are used interchangeably.

Let's define them:

- 'Digitisation is the process of converting information into a digital format.'
- 'Digitalisation is the use of digital technologies to change a business model and provide new value-producing opportunities; it is the process of moving to a digital business.'

Now let's speak English.

Scanning your supermarket shopping bills is digitising your bills from the squiggly long checkout bills to neatly stored images on your phone or computer.

So, this is digitisation – it's the 'what'.

Getting a program/app that reads all your scanned supermarket bills for a month (big data) and tells you:

- I recommend you buy your meats from the butcher on Main Street – it is fresher and about 23 per cent cheaper.
- Your consumption of fruits is decreasing – eat more greens for a healthier diet.
- I didn't know you liked chocolate-covered pretzels so much.
- You buy too much junk food, buddy; we need to talk.

And this is digitalisation – it's the 'how'.

So, digitisation is the first step in realising digitalisation.

Clear as mud?

Post # 100

Leadership is not about barking orders

#Thisiswhatticklesme

Coming back from the deep freezer in Toronto (−20C) to sunny Dubai (+25C), I sat next to a bubbly and enthusiastic young chap who was a chatterbox.

He asked 20 questions/min, and one of them was the clichéd 'What is leadership?'

We agreed that because my eyes were seeing double, I would post something on LinkedIn and tag him.

So here it is from many years of experience, practice, and observation.

Leadership is *not* about:

- Being high and mighty (arrogant and condescending)
- Barking orders and pretending to know everything

- Telling your people, 'Because I am the boss and you're not'

Leadership *is* being able to communicate like your mother, that is:

- Tell stories to move and inspire
- Encourage, teach, and show direction
- Give you a kick in the derrière when you need it every once in a while, and repeat

So next time you see (or think of) your mother, take a bow and say, 'Thank you'.

Post # 101

I don't get vegan-ism

#Thisiswhatticklesme

No doubt, diet is a hot topic. There is a lot of debate out there, and there was a good discussion on my last post on being a flexitarian.

I subscribe to and understand all sorts of diets: vegetarian, flexitarian, and various other short-period weight-loss diets like the ketogenic diet, the Zone diet, raw-food diet, etc. . . .

But one diet I can't understand is vegan-ism.

My questions are:

- Is our food chain ready for it?
- Can a low-income family afford a strict vegan diet/lifestyle at home?
- Is it really more motivated by health or by animal cruelty?
- Is it possible for a vegan to buy breakfast without asking 17 questions?

Khaled M. Ismail

I used to have a colleague who was a committed vegan. It was a nightmare going out with her for lunch or dinner.

What tickled me was, almost every time, we would have to call the restaurant a couple of times before we arrived, and when there, we would end up visiting and befriending the chef in the kitchen (unless the word 'vegan' was in the name of the restaurant, which are a handful in each city).

Try hosting a vegan at home, without having a crisis or having them bring their own vegan food and wine (yes, there is vegan wine).

Please share your thoughts!

Post # 102

92 per cent of people fail at keeping their New Year's resolutions

#Thisiswhatticklesme

Somebody asked me today, 'So what's your New Year's resolution?' This question tickles me because I am not a big fan of New Year resolutions.

I have been there, done that, and got the T-shirt – a couple of times . . .

With good intentions, most of us make the same list of New Year's resolutions every year (they are mostly weight, money, or health related).

We get super excited the first couple of days – three weeks tops – and then they're dropped one by one like hot potatoes – and all is forgotten (even that expensive gym membership).

FYI, 92 per cent of people fail at keeping their New Year's resolutions!

My advice: Forget about the New Year's resolution gobbledygook!

From experience: Whatever you want to do, be 100 per cent unequivocally committed to it, and do *'whatever it takes'* to achieve it – at any time of the year.

You *must* be prepared to sacrifice something to get towards your goals.

What's your New Year's resolution?

Happy New Year, everybody!

Post # 103

You used to forget you had a job

#Thisiswhatticklesme

'Tis the season when many of us go on holidays. I remember the days when we didn't have e-mails. When you went on vacation, you *really* went on vacation!

You switched off completely! You even forgot you had a job.

But you came back to a dizzying pile of work.

Then came e-mail and Nokia 8210 (my first cool mobile phone) – I can still remember the ringtone.

I Want This Back During Vacation!

When you went on vacation, you went on vacation – no e-mails, a couple of text messages, with the occasional call, and plenty of voice mails.

But when you came back, you panicked at the number of e-mails in your inbox. It used to take me about a week to catch up.

Now we have a smartphone, which is raining e-mails and notifications every couple of minutes.

When I go on vacation, I try, but I can't fully switch off. My life is *on* my phone and *in* my e-mails . . . (friends, banks, airlines, shopping, etc.)

So, to pretend that I will not look at my e-mails is a big lie.

I am always peeking.

What tickles me is that now I come back from vacation fully up to date with no pending e-mails in my inbox . . . sad but true. I do check and respond to e-mails during vacation but at intervals.

I envy people who can switch *on* their 'out of office' and switch *off* completely.

What's your e-mail strategy during vacation?

Image source: Nokia

Post # 104

Happy whatever doesn't offend you!

#Thisiswhatticklesme

I am feeling a little festive, but tickled at the same time. In some parts of the world, some people are deprived of celebrating their holidays properly!

I was talking to a dear friend who lives and works at a school in snowy Travisland. She made reference with envy to a recent post I made with a Christmas tree in Dubai featured in it.

'Nice tree; we are not allowed to have one at our school!' she said.

'Why?' I asked.

'Because the school board felt that could be viewed as insensitive and could offend some of our students who are not celebrating Christmas,' she said.

'So, what do you celebrate?' I asked.

'Not sure.' She shrugged . . .

PS. I couldn't see the shrug over the phone, but I felt it.

It tickles me that in this day and age, we still don't accept and appreciate diversity and celebrate each other's holidays, like Ramadan, Eid, Diwali, Christmas, Hanukkah . . .

And be able to say:

Eid Mubarak, Happy Diwali, or Merry Christmas to each other (regardless of which faith you belong to), instead of the watered-down 'Season's Greetings' or 'Happy Holidays'.

Call me progressive!

Merry Christmas tree for everyone.

PS. I hope I didn't offend anyone with this post!

Post # 105

Try the 3:00 AM test

#Thisiswhatticklesme

During the weekend, I overheard someone at our table bragging about how well connected he was and how many friends he had. I knew he was a bit of a 'trumpet blower', so I asked:

'How many friends do you really, really have?'

'Many!' he responded, with a whiff of arrogance.

'How many can you feel comfortable asking to borrow US$1,000 from *and* get it?'

Pause . . . (I thought he was going to level with me and come to his senses.)

'Many!' he replied.

'OK,' I thought, 'maybe money isn't the best gauge.'

'How many would you call at 3:00 AM if you were in an emergency?'

Long pause . . . followed by a smirk (the penny dropped).

What tickles me is that with today's fast-paced digital world, some of us get confused between real friends, friendly acquaintances, and social media connections.

From experience, friendships are diamond rare and ticklingly special – hold on to them dearly, like you would to your smartphone.

How many friends can you call at 3:00 AM?

BTW, can I borrow US$1,000?

Post # 106

Overdose of ho, ho, ho!

#Thisiswhatticklesme

'Tis the season to be jolly and to decorate the heck out of everything, from home interiors and exteriors to mall and hotel lobbies, with Christmas trees and all the sparkly trimmings.

The top three things that tickle me during this season:

1. The overdose of events, gatherings, and parties that fill the calendar for a month and the amount of food and drink I consume during this period – which takes me the rest of the year to get rid of.
2. The barrage of Christmas music – *Jingle Bells*, *All I Want for Christmas Is You*, and *I Am Dreaming of a White Christmas* – to the point that I start having dreams, starring Santa and Rudolph the Red-Nosed Reindeer.
3. And the one that tickles me the most is when I get friends and family from the other side of the world wishing me 'Season's Greetings' and asking me if we have Christmas trees in Dubai . . . I giggle and

Khaled M. Ismail

> send them a picture of the biggest Christmas tree in the world.

Ho, ho, ho!

What tickles you during Christmas season?

Post # 107

Image source: *Montreal Times*

#Thisiswhatticklesme

In Montréal, you can no longer say 'Hi' to me! Only 'Bonjour'. Montréal is a beautiful multicultural city that my family has called home for more than 30 years!

People in Montréal speak perfect English and French . . . actually, their French is in some ways more authentic (e.g., Stop signs in FR say 'Stop'; in Québec they say 'Arrêt').

Politicians in Montréal were bored! So, they decided to tackle a *major* problem.

Khaled M. Ismail

Last week, the Quebec's National Assembly debated and unanimously adopted a motion calling on store clerks to stick with a simple 'Bonjour' when greeting customers, instead of Montréal's usual 'Bonjour/Hi'.

Framing poor little 'Hi' as a threat to the French language... really!

What tickles me is that no change management guru or consultant has managed to help the Québec government with their constant attempts to pass effective language laws to protect the French language.

To win the people over, instead of scaring them with another law or motion, I recommend issuing this statement:

> Bonjour, people! French is a beautiful language, and 'Bonjour' is a musical greeting that differentiates our city and province; give it a try! S'il vous plait.

And leave people to greet each other in whichever sign or language they want!

Post # 108

Build it, and they will come! Dubai

#Thisiswhatticklesme

I am either getting sentimental in my wiser years, or I am just more appreciative of fabulous achievements.

Fifteen years ago . . . almost *every* single high-rise in Dubai did *not* exist.

The bravery and tenacity of this city (Dubai) are inspirational.

I now believe in the saying – adapted from the 1989 movie *Field of Dreams*:

> If you build it, *they* will come.

I liked the saying, but I wasn't sure who 'they' were.

What tickles me is that I used to sarcastically question:

Khaled M. Ismail

'Are they mad?'

'Why are they building all those buildings, the metro system, the 14-lane highways, the largest airport and the tallest building in the world, and for whom?'

They proved me wrong!

This drive and spirit of 'Let's just do it' is now embedded in how I think, because I have witnessed it all – its highs, bubbles, and lows – and I have learnt from it.

Happy National Day, United Arab Emirates – 2 December.

Post # 109

'~~Our~~ BlackMotion ~~range combines lighter materials, enhanced aerodynamics, economical engines, and tyres that create less friction, which~~ saves you ~~fuel and can reduce your tax, which means you will have more~~ money,' said car company X.

#Thisiswhatticklesme

I just love this quote:

If I had more time, I would have written a shorter letter.
—Blaise Pascal

Developing a clear and simple message, e-mail, advert, or presentation is *hard* and requires more effort, but well worth it if you want to engage and connect with people.

So many of us get sucked into the shop language, departmental lingo, and industry jargon that we sometime lose the audience along the way because they simply don't know.

All they care about is 'What is your message?' and 'What's in it for me?'

It so tickles me when I receive a lengthy newspaper-like e-mail or a lengthy presentation, and halfway through it, I start to think about what's for lunch. I 'sometimes' stop myself from responding with:

'So, what do you really, really want from me or wish to give me in the end?'

Simple is beautiful.

If one day you're feeling naughty and want to complicate life and spice things up, use this fun 'Complex Sentence Generator'. Google csgenerator.com.

Post # 110

1 trophy for you
10 trophies for me

#Thisiswhatticklesme

I now have a renewed respect for award events/programmes for any industry. The effort that goes into the submissions is commendable, and the creativity/innovation is inspiring.

Having recently been involved in an award event as a judge, and as a spectator at an award ceremony, I have some tickling observations:

- The submission format (form) is antiquated – very lengthy and at times difficult to follow.
- The videos created to describe the entries are absolutely fab and, I am guessing, cost a pretty penny – without which I wouldn't have understood at least one-third of the entries.
- The overall process, even though fair, is a little opaque – it was for me.

- The # of categories are growing and are intertwined – you can easily submit an entry into four to five categories.
- Who has the time to prepare and submit all these entries?

But what tickles me is that this process – if you have a *good* product – can be a numbers game – like the lottery.

One company submitted more than 35 per cent of the entries, paid an arm and a leg for their submission, and won a truckload of the awards.

I say, 'Well done and congratulations to them' – as long as the system is the way it is. I would do exactly the same and make sure my offices are splattered with trophies to show them off.

I am not going to win an award for this post, am I?

Post # 111

OK wait, let me ask my mother!

#Thisiswhatticklesme

Today was another sunny weekend day in Dubai. (Surprise!) I was sipping on my morning coffee, and suddenly my phone rang.

'Hello, Mr. Ismail, this is Travis from your bank, Travisbank Ltd., and this call may be recorded for quality purposes.'

It all sounded very official and legit.

I usually just say, 'No, thank you', even before they launch into their spiel because I don't want to waste their time or mine.

But today was different! I was chillaxing, drinking my coffee, and decided to hear their amazing offer.

'We have a great promotion where you can take out money on your credit card at an amazing low rate of *x*.'

Clearly, this offer doesn't apply to me because I don't even have a credit card with this bank!

I said to Travis, 'OK wait, let me ask my mother!'

What tickles me is that this is not the first time I got this sort of call. Banks outsource these promotions to tele-marketers without giving them access to their database.

They knew nothing about me!

Some banks still like the good old-fashioned way of doing business, despite having enough data about me (including my shoe size). What happened to big data and CRM with banks?

I put Travis on hold for a min whilst making my second cup of coffee and then came back with:

'My mother said *no*!'

Beep, beep, beep . . .

Post # 112

With me . . . you're gonna get sick of winning

#Thisiswhatticklesme

'With me, you're gonna get sick of *winning*!' said a well-known person; let's call him 'Travis'. He and I don't seem to like the same ice cream flavour.

There is nothing wrong with a winning attitude, a positive and optimistic outlook on life.

I subscribe to it – but don't take it too far, because there are consequences to winning all the time.

Today, I was out to get some ice cream; I saw two people argue and almost fistfight over a parking spot!

Seriously!

I thought to myself! Is it worth it?

My answer was, with chocolate ice cream dripping on my hand, 'Nah! Life's too short for this kind of rubbish.' Slurp!

What tickles me is some mature people still don't appreciate the golden rule of relationships, negotiations, and engagement:

>Choose Your Battles.

Over time, I learnt that in any relationship and interaction:

- You have to win some and lose some.
- If you insist on winning every single time, and others lose, you'll create enemies, and people won't want to deal with you.
- Compromise is a more sustainable outcome, a.k.a., a win/win.
- *Don't Sweat the Small Stuff* – a great book by Richard Carlson.

Post # 113

Don't you dare ask them for a change or critique their work the wrong way

#Thisiswhatticklesme

This will make you think! I started my career in advertising when it was cool with a dash of 'je n'est sais quoi'. I have very fond memories, where I learnt a lot about how to manage people and bring ideas to life to sell stuff.

One thing I vividly remember is having to deal with the creative people. I discovered and learnt the hard way that dealing with creatives can be a bit tickling and requires special skills . . . like walking on eggshells.

Working with 'left-brained' (analytical) versus 'right-brained' (creative) people has different sets of rules.

They are visual, complex, passionate, emotional, temperamental, and somewhat impulsive.

I learnt that briefing them or giving them feedback is an art form. Don't you dare ask them for a change, or critique their work the wrong way. You need them to 'like' you first, if you want them to give you a little of their magic.

I subsequently learnt that creative people don't only exist in ad agencies . . . they are all around us, in marketing and fashion – they can be artists, stylists, chefs, architects . . .

And the same rules apply to how to manage them.

They like to daydream, brainstorm, be praised, and have time for solitude, people watch, mindfulness.

How do you deal with the creative geniuses in your life?

Post # 114

Have I stumbled upon a masterpiece?

#Thisiswhatticklesme

I was recently invited to a highfalutin opening event of an art gallery. I was thrilled that I was even invited, but then when I got there, I was a little tickled by what I saw.

I am not your typical artist type, but I sure do like and appreciate a good piece of art when I see one.

What really tickled me was when I saw a simple piece of paper folded with a paperclip!

Oh, oh, and a black line . . .

I thought art was a form of creativity and an expression of feelings, like love or anger, of beauty . . .

What is this an expression of?

I subsequently saw a ripped piece of carpet and thought to myself, 'Have I stumbled upon a masterpiece?'

Post # 115

Ask 'why' several times? Just don't answer yourself

#Thisiswhatticklesme

I once took philosophy in university, and, being a pragmatist, this subject was a bit hazy and tickling for me.

I started to appreciate philosophy as I grew older, and I must add 'wiser' . . . even though some of it still tickles me a little.

Philosophy is defined as the study of general and fundamental problems concerning matters such as existence, knowledge, values, reason, mind, and language . . . by repeatedly asking one simple tickling question: Why?

Philosophy does not exist in business unless you are a realist!

In business, for me, philosophy translated itself to the concept of the '5 Whys', and I am starting to like it because it helps me solve problems and see things differently.

'5 Whys' is one of many root-cause analysis tools to quickly get to the cause of an issue before jumping into fixing mode!

Try it . . . ask 'Why' several times before you do something in your business or everyday life.

Your lens on the world will change!

Even though you might come across as tickling as hell to your friends and colleagues.

That was a bit too deep for me!

Post # 116

If I have US$2 million

#Thisiswhatticklesme

How much is enough? Really?

This month, 20 years ago, I was driving in a beat-up car with a friend; let's call him Mr. T.

He said, 'If I had US$100,000, I would leave my job and open a shack-type bar by the sea and live in Mykonos.'

Mr. T progressed to be a successful corporate guy and then turned tech entrepreneur.

Again, 10 years ago this month (his birthday), we talked about his retirement plan and reminisced about his Mykonos shack.

He then said, 'If I had US$2 million, I would buy a simple house with a pool by the sea in Sardinia and have BBQs and parties every day and just retire.'

#Thisiswhatticklesme

This week, we talked again, and he announced, 'I am working on a deal, and if I close it, I will walk away with US$10 million. I will buy a seaside mansion in St. Tropez and my dream car and just catch the rays and chill!'

I said 'Really? What happened to retiring with the shack and the simple house idea?'

It tickled me when he responded, 'The more I have, the more I spend because I need to keep my living standards!'

I said, 'Would you really retire if you close this deal?'

He said, 'We'll see,' with a smirk on his face.

We – most of us, at least – are a bunch of ambitious and greedy creatures! We are never satisfied.

How much do you need to retire?

Post # 117

'Thank you'
And
'You're an idiot'

#Thisiswhatticklesme

When someone asks me how I am doing, my usual answer (not always) is:

'I am absolutely *marvellous*!'

It works for me and puts others in a more positive frame of mind.

Yes, words can easily affect our mood and have a contagious effect. Try spending five minutes with a chronic whiner who is never happy and complains about everything. There is a high chance that you'll feel your energy deflated.

Japanese scientist, Dr. Masaru Emoto tested the power of spoken words.

#Thisiswhatticklesme

He placed two cups of cooked white rice in two separate jars and fixed the lids in place, labelling one jar 'Thank You' and the other, 'You're an idiot'.

The jars were left in a school classroom, and the students were instructed to say the words on the labels *to* the corresponding jars, twice a day.

After 30 days, the rice in the jar that was constantly insulted had shrivelled into a black, gelatinous mass.

The rice in the jar that was thanked was as white and fluffy as the day it was made.

What tickles me is if words have this effect on a jar of rice, what the heck does it do to people?

I still witness people using negative, insulting, and derogatory language and expect people around them to be productive and happy.

Words have great power; choose them wisely!

Do you agree?

Post # 118

Hello, my name is Kal!

#Thisiswhatticklesme

Looking for a job? Please take note . . .

I am usually not controversial in my posts, nor do I intend to start.

My posts are mainly about important everyday topics, written in an informative and entertaining way, with a sprinkle of humour.

This contentious topic was brought to my attention by a young man who was looking for a job in Travisland!

He presented the *exact* same CV with two different names: A (his real name) and B (a borrowed name).

'B' got the job!

This tickles me immensely.

#Thisiswhatticklesme

There are plenty of articles, studies, and research on the subject out there . . .

Some findings include:

1. Job applications in British cities from people with white-sounding names were 74 per cent more likely to receive a positive response than applications from people with an ethnic-minority name.
2. French-sounding names received 70 per cent more call-backs than the other four names – two of North African origin, and two that sounded foreign but were hard to place.
3. The résumés with white-sounding names spurred 50 per cent more call-backs than the ones with black-sounding names.
4. Have a foreign-sounding name? Change it to get a job!

Sincerely yours,
KAL

Post # 119

CRM blew my cover!

#Thisiswhatticklesme

I have a nosy friend; let's call him Ignatius, or 'Iggy' for short. Iggy is a successful connector, a socialite, a salesman extraordinaire, and a curious guy.

He has a tickling habit of calling the restaurant where he is going for dinner and checking out who is on the booking list . . . so he can prepare his pitches and do his homework.

Last week I called in to make a reservation for six, and I was recognised by my phone #. 'Hello, Mr. Ismail, how may I help you? The usual table?'

I thought, 'Hmm, this restaurant's CRM system is an impressively oiled machine – works like a charm, and I feel important!'

I said, 'A table for six under the name "Travis", please,' trying to go undercover to avoid Iggy's nosiness.

After a slight hesitation, I heard 'OK, done!'

24 hours later . . . Iggy calls me and says, 'Looking forward to seeing you tomorrow night; b.t.w., who is coming with you?'

Hmm, I learnt two things from this episode:

1. CRM is good for personalising your experience, good for business and your ego, but can easily 'blow your cover'.
2. Tipping trumps confidentiality! (Iggy's specialty).

In conclusion: Iggy joined our table during dessert and became friends with the two couples on my table.

You gotta love CRM and admire Iggy's tenaciousness!

Post # 120

Graffiti – Philadelphia – 1967

#Thisiswhatticklesme

Every profession has its gurus, legends, and stars. It's the pioneers, the daring, the fearless, but also the talented that stand out.

One profession that has intrigued me since childhood is art and artists.

More specifically, graffiti art!

I recently visited Johannesburg, which is known for its graffiti – I met a graffiti artist; let's call him 'Travis'. I was tickled about what I learnt from him:

- The first graffiti was done in 1967 by Cornbread, a high school student from Philadelphia, who started tagging city walls to get the attention of a girl. (Girls are the cause of our evolution.)

#Thisiswhatticklesme

- There are some world-famous graffiti artists like Banksy, Dondi, Shepard Fairey, Lady Pink, Blek le Rat, Mr. Brainwash . . .
- It is illegal in most cities; artists risk punishment and possible jail time, which is why most go with their 'street'/tagging names.
- Some graffiti artists are political, and some are egotistical, as most draw/tag their names.
- There is a lot of culture, and many coded messages, hidden in their work.

So mysterious and so tickling!

When I grow up, I wanna be a graffiti artist.

Post # 121

Eyes . . . Spill the beans

#Thisiswhatticklesme

Your eyes! They speak. They reveal so much about you. You can't 'shut them up' unless you're asleep.

Some say, 'Eyes are the window to the soul.' So romantic!

Is it?

They convey your happiness, anger, disgust, fear, sadness, love, seduction . . .

What's tickling is the number of *secrets* your *pupils* reveal.

Pupils will either constrict or dilate depending on your emotion or state of mind.

If you like something or someone, your pupils will dilate, and if you are turned off, they will constrict.

Skilled salespeople look for the size of the pupils when selling/negotiating with you. If they see a fully dilated pupil, they know not to budge . . . 'cause you're a 'home run', a 'done deal', a 'slam dunk' sale.

Next time you're talking to someone, pay attention to the size of their pupils.

(*Please* don't go right up to their face and stare – that's just weird).

They will tell you what excites them; they may also tell you if they like you . . . and if they'll do business with you, or not!

Remember: People do business with people they like!

Gaze responsibly!

Post # 122

This one felt softer

#Thisiswhatticklesme

Since it is now trendy to do 'social experiments', I decided to do one yesterday – so I don't feel left out – in collaboration with an awesome salesperson/actor.

I offered a friend – let's call him 'Travis' – to choose from three identical white cotton shirts of the same brand with three different clearly marked price tags.

- Shirt A = US$29.99
- Shirt B = US$50
- Shirt C = US$99

With a little help from the sales actor, Travis gravitated towards the better-quality option.

Which option do you think Travis preferred?
A, B, or C?

Maybe the question is rhetorical.

#Thisiswhatticklesme

Actual results will be revealed shortly after checking with the consultants and tabulating all the analytics, along with Travis' rationale and the science behind it.

Initial results were of a tickling nature!

Post # 123

He preferred the 'posh' option

#Thisiswhatticklesme – Social Experiment part #2

- Shirt A = US$29.99
- Shirt B = US$50
- Shirt C = US$99

After extensive analysis and review of the analytics, here are the results:

Executive Summary
Travis preferred option C ($99), the 'posh' option.

Detailed analysis:
He initially liked all three shirts equally and couldn't tell much difference, but once the sales actor revealed the prices, Travis started leaning towards option C.

Travis felt that the fabric on option C had 'a softer feel to it and the white was a bit brighter'.

I asked him, 'Is option C (US$99) really 3× better quality than option A (US$29.99)?' He fidgeted a little and hesitated to answer.

His brain was playing games with him.

What really tickled me was when Travis found out the trick and discovered that all three shirts were exactly identical and came from the same shelf . . . he decided to pick the shirt with the fake US$99 price tag, even though he paid US$50 to buy it (the actual price).

Conclusion: According to 'real' research, pricing has a huge impact on how we interpret the experience. We tend to associate cost with quality and value.

This is also true for food, drinks, and, particularly, wine.

Final words: Pricing strategies matter, margins make the world go around; just don't be a sucker for high prices.

Post # 124

Hire me, 'cause I work good!

#Thisiswhatticklesme

No one is born a lawyer, a plumber, a doctor, an engineer, or a marketer – no one. We're all born jobless and in diapers! No interests or profession.

We grow, learn, grow some more, and continue to learn . . . develop interests, and discover passions.

Then life hits you! You discover that you *need* a job to live, to survive, to have a meaningful life.

After many years of observation, I discovered that the toughest job in the world – besides being a parent – is actually looking for a job – for the right job.

For some, it can be stressful, sleepless nights, a roller-coaster ride – one day you are up and the next day you are in the dumps, and your confidence is tested daily.

#Thisiswhatticklesme

I get endless messages and e-mails from people looking for a job. I empathise. We've all been there . . . and I try to help when I can.

What tickles me is how some people don't take this job seriously; they're so blasé about it.

- 'Looking for a job, look at the profile.'
- 'Hey, can I apply for a job at your company?'
- 'I don't have experience in X, can I apply anyway?'
- 'I hear you pay well . . . do you have any open positions?'

And the winner is,

- 'I am applying for the advertised job; I can't remember the title.'

I am usually not, but now I'm speechless.
Please take this job seriously. End of rant.

Post # 125

Elon Musk stole my idea

#Thisiswhatticklesme

Elon Musk is not a genius; he is an 'actionary'. I thought about travelling by rocket before he did.

While growing up, I went to many boarding schools – Beirut (Choueifat) and all over Europe (Beau-Soliel and Tasis). So, I was on airplanes all the time, going home for every break and for the summers.

I used to daydream!

On one occasion I had a vision that one day we would travel in a rocket, a little faster than the DC 10 I used to travel on.

What tickles me is that Elon Musk stole my idea. The only difference is he made it happen (almost/coming soon).

HONG KONG TO SINGAPORE IN 22 MIN, LONDON TO DUBAI OR NEW YORK IN 29 MIN.

#Thisiswhatticklesme

Most people's daily commute time to work is more than 30 min.

Elon Musk is an action visionary! (actionary) – 'not a shareholder', but a man who makes crazy ideas come to life. He is a hustler who's been to hell and back (almost bankrupt several times). His list of achievements is incredible (PayPal, SolarCity, Tesla, SpaceX, Hyperloop concept, etc.).

One day, before I 'go' and start pushing up daisies, I want to have breakfast in Sydney, a stopover in Dubai for a cup of tea, have lunch in Mayfair in London, and then head off to Toronto for dinner with my daughter.

Where would you go in a day if you could travel this fast?

Post # 126

Chances are you will live to 70

#Thisiswhatticklesme

If you are less than 35 years old, please stop reading – no need to depress you, yet. All others, let's talk about the inevitable.

The average life expectancy now is ~71 years (68 for Travis and 72 for Helga).

What tickles me is that we are the only living creatures in this universe (per my scientific knowledge) who actually *know* that we are going to die, yet we behave like we are immortal.

We fight over land, objects, and religions; get angry and lose our temper over the littlest things, and for what?

Some accumulate and save so much money that it could outlast them several lives over. Why?

Travis even bets big money with the Life Insurance Co. – that he's *not* going to die.

Insurance Co. bets bigger money that he *is*.

Travis *wins* and dies . . .

So, your 'Immortality Project' should be to do good, be nice to others, and leave a legacy to be remembered by, 'cause you ain't gonna be around for too long!

If you wish to extend your stay, may I suggest that you eat well and move to Okinawa – home of the highest life expectancy in the world.

The Okinawan diet, low in calories and high in micronutrients, is our path to longevity. Scientists found that mice on calorie-restricted diets similar to that of the Okinawans have remarkable lifespan extensions.

What one-sentence legacy do you want to be remembered by?

Post # 127

1N73LL1G3NC3
15 7h3
4 B1L17Y
70 4D4P7 70
CH4NG3

#Thisiswhatticklesme

I am fascinated by how intelligent people are – when they want to be! Our brain works in such mysterious and wonderful ways.

Some people are quick learners, and some are as thick as a four-foot wall. In some ways, it's a choice or a lack of interest . . . the latter bunch tickles me.

When I was growing up, if I did not catch on quickly to something (was disinterested), my dear mother would say, 'Don't be a donkey' – of course, in a loving way – and I am not traumatised.

#Thisiswhatticklesme

But then I soon learnt that even donkeys can be 'smart', or in other words, can learn patterns.

I watched a donkey in 'Travisland' get loaded with goodies in location A and sent off to destination B, and it returned, all by itself . . . several times a day.

Talking about patterns, if you can read the sentence above, give yourself a 'high five'. Well done, bravo! Your brain just picked up a pattern and adapted to make meaning out of this sentence.

This is a quote by 573PH3N H4WK1NG.

When you figure out what it says, just post the word 'Travis' in the comments. Don't spell it out. Give others a chance.

So, this is how we learn!

H4V3 4 F4N74571C D4Y

Post # 128

E Pluribus Unum

#Thisiswhatticklesme

I thought I was multilingual until I recently met someone – let's call him 'Travis' – who spoke seven languages fluently. He was annoyingly impressive.

That is seven more opportunities to work and connect with different people.

Every language = Another person.

I was tickled when Travis told me that I possibly understand a little of another language . . . without knowing it.

That language is Latin. I discovered that Latin is all around us, and I use some of it without knowing!

Like:
- Veni, vidi, vici = I came, I saw, I conquered
- Veni, vidi, amavi = I came, I saw, I loved
- Veritas = Truth (Can be found on Harvard's logo)

#Thisiswhatticklesme

- E pluribus unum = Out of many, one (This phrase was once the United States' motto)
- Carpe diem = Seize the day
- Novus ordo seclorum = A new order of the ages – can be found on a US$1 bill
- Impromptu = Spontaneous or without preparation
- Quid pro quo = Of equal exchange or substitution
- Per se = In itself, intrinsically, of an inherent nature
- Ad hoc = For one specific case/purpose
- Bona fide = Unquestionable, in good faith
- Pro rata = Proportionally, in equal parts
- Pro bono = Work done without charge

End of Latin lesson #1

Practice #1
Mihi Vellicare Patiar Vos = ?

How many languages do you speak?

Post # 129

I am feeling goooooood!

#Thisiswhatticklesme

Good is relative! Does 'Good Morning' really mean that you are having a 'good' morning, or are you really wishing someone a 'good' morning? Hmm.

Enough with the philosophical stuff!

'Good' comes in different shapes and sizes! 'Good' is usually positive and optimistic. Sure, things can be great, excellent, and wonderful, but 'good' is the foundation, not the enemy.

I don't introduce my imaginary friend Travis as 'my excellent friend', but as 'my "good" friend'. We may have an excellent relationship.

We also use the word 'good' in so many contexts . . . usually in happy and bright ways, like:

- I am feeling 'Good' – Nina Simone
- 'Good' stuff!

- All 'good'
- 'Good' job
- The 'good' old days
- The 'good', the bad, and the . . .
- 'Good'ness gracious

What tickles me is people also do 'good'! They do lots of little 'good' things and deeds to each other every day.

It sometimes goes unnoticed by the receiver, but mostly by the person who's doing 'good'!

Appreciate the people who do 'good' for you. They'll love it and do more.

Are you feeling 'gooood'?

Post # 130

Do you need a wake-up call?

#Thisiswhatticklesme

I was staying in a hotel recently, and before I went to bed, I phoned the reception. 'Hi, this is Room 212. Can I have a wake-up call, please?'

The receptionist, let's call him 'Travis', replied:

> Yes. You sleep late, you don't exercise enough, you are a bit unfit, you can do with a healthier diet, you are losing your hair, and what's left is getting grey; you're a tad OCD, you're sometimes 'penny wise and pound foolish', you're getting fussier and more impatient in your old age, your #Thisiswhatticklesme posts suck, you don't call your mother often enough . . . would you like that for 7:00 or 7:30?

#Thisiswhatticklesme

Beep, beep, beep . . . he tickled me; I hung up on him, obviously.

Wouldn't you want a Travis in your life, to give you a 'wake-up' call every once in a while?

Who is your Travis?

Post # 131

Please don't ask for 'Discount'; he doesn't work here anymore

#Thisiswhatticklesme

In some countries, it's a way of life. Some cultures can't do business without it. Haggling is not for everyone. Some people are good at it; some people hate it.

I don't mind it at all; in fact, I think of it as a national sport.

I know someone who would rather bungee jump, without a rope, than ask for a discount even from a carpet salesman.

I was recently tickled when I was at a souvenir shop. I asked for the 'bestest' price, and the hurried, skinny, and bearded salesman pointed at this witty sign in his shop window, which made me chuckle. It read 'Please don't ask for "Discount"; he doesn't work here anymore.'

#Thisiswhatticklesme

I still asked for and got a 'volume' discount – because I bought not one but two stuffed elephants and a fridge magnet.

Many establishments have their own fancy pricing policies – depending on the season and how much they like your face.

I happen to have a fancier policy of my own, 'Ask, and you shall receive – sometimes!'

What's yours?

Post # 132

Husband Day Care Centre

#Thisiswhatticklesme

They looked after me. There was no hitting, verbal or physical abuse, and I got a certificate. The only problem was that their Wi-Fi was too slow.

At the 'Cape Town Husband Day Care Centre', they provide you with comfy couches, big-screen TVs, and ample food and beverages – the distilled and fermented type – until you are picked up feeling a little numb and too happy for your own good.

What a novel business model, which caters to a desperate captive audience, one I will pitch to the local malls.

#Thisiswhatticklesme

What tickled me most was: What if they imposed a policy where you wouldn't be allowed out until your spouse returned to check you out?!

What's their policy if she doesn't return?

Would you check him in?

Post # 133

A person who feels appreciated will always do more than expected

#Thisiswhatticklesme

Look Travis in the eyes, make him feel valued, and show him some love! Then sit back, and watch the sparkles in his eyes.

I learnt that appreciation is a fundamental human need and that people respond to appreciation because it confirms they are valued. It also drives motivation and productivity – it's a miracle.

Appreciation and recognition come in different shapes and sizes:

- Write Travis a handwritten thank-you note (an SMS or WhatsApp is less powerful, but you may if you must).
- Say 'Well done' or 'Outstanding work' – be genuine.

- Whisper 'Travis, you impressed me.'
- Chocolates, flowers, and cupcakes also work beautifully – be generous.

What tickles me is that people take people for granted and expect them to be motivated and happy.

Appreciation is the most underutilised *force* in the world; let's use it more often (me too!)

A little secret: When you appreciate someone, you feel good too!

Who is worth being appreciated?

Post # 134

Technology is scaring me

#Thisiswhatticklesme

It is highly recommended that you don't say everything you're thinking. So many times, I want to tell someone how I really feel about them, but I bite my tongue and give them the politically correct answer.

Can you imagine what I'd say to my colleague Travis who continuously talks rubbish or who has body odour and I have to sit next to him in a meeting?

It won't be pretty or appropriate.

Technology is becoming ticklingly scary, as it can now detect so much about you!

There are security cameras, which by scanning up to 50–60 points on your face, can detect if you're angry, stressed, or nervous – they are soon coming to a smartphone near you.

#Thisiswhatticklesme

There is a new technology called EQ-Radio, which sends wireless signals that reflect off a person's body and back to the device. Its beat-extraction algorithms break the reflections into individual heartbeats and analyse the small variations in heartbeat from the wireless signal at an accuracy comparable to on-body ECG monitors.

And what tickles me is now there is an algorithm that can tell whether you're gay or straight, from a photograph!

So soon we won't be able to hide our thoughts, emotions, or feelings towards something or someone.

All they have to do is scan our face or send a wireless signal.

Boy, am I in trouble!

Post # 135

The ugly fine print

#Thisiswhatticklesme

Why can't we just have straightforward honest transactions anymore, without the hidden costs and the ambush of the fine print?

I was trying to cancel a service with an existing provider today, and I was told, 'There is a cancellation fee of US$25.'

I said, 'If you charge me the US$25, I will cancel my subscription altogether. I wasn't told of this fee when I signed up.'

'But it's in the contract; additional fees *may* apply at the discretion of the company,' they said.

I said, 'Well, they *may* not apply to me!'

After more than 10 min of argument and speaking to the manager, and they agreed to waive the fee.

I was truly tickled!

Why can't we compete honestly and with the final price!

I come across all sorts of fees:

- Booking and rebooking fee
- Transaction fee
- Cancellation fee
- Renewal fee
- Maintenance fee
- Administration fee
- Speaking-to-an-operator fee
- Tax-refund fee

Airlines are notorious for this:

- Printing-airline-ticket fee
- Booking-a-seat fee
- Checked and carry-on baggage fee
- Blanket fees
- In-flight entertainment fees (Thankfully, we don't have 'Staring at a blank screen' fee)
- Fuel-surcharge fee

And the one that tickles me:

- Obesity fee (Yes, some airlines will charge you extra if you don't have a six pack)

Do all these fees tickle you too, or is it just me?

Post # 136

WTF*

#Thisiswhatticklesme

We've all used it at some point. Some use it multiple times an hour in every other sentence. Some use it as a personal style to come across as authentic/raw/unedited.

If you say you've never used it . . . you are . . .

Yes, I am talking about profanity – foul language, the 'F-word' and all its entourage of words and translations.

Sometimes it is used to express 'macho-ness', other times to express anger or dissatisfaction. It can also be used as a term of endearment.

What tickles me is when it is used as a filler between words at the workplace. (I am not talking about having the soundtrack of *Goodfellas* playing in the background.)

In some companies, profanity is common and accepted – it depends on the culture. Some argue that it improves your career – 'lighten up'. In other companies, it is grounds for termination.

I am no angel; I have used it scarcely and selectively, both inside and outside the workplace – but I don't like it.

If Travis uses profanity at work on a regular basis, I would either ask him to *stop it* or cringe and distance myself.

In some countries, using profanity is illegal and is punishable by law; in others, it is part of their 'freedom of speech'.

What is your view on using profanity at work?

*WTF = Wow, That's Fantastic.

Post # 137

What gives you goose bumps?

#Thisiswhatticklesme

Unless you like Montréal on a windy February night, it is such a good and tickling feeling when you get goose bumps.

Goose bumps are a reflex initiated by the sympathetic nervous system. So, it is all about experiencing a strong emotion.

During a recent briefing to our agency, we filled the usual creative brief, answering all the routine questions that Travis, the creative, would like to know:

Objectives, channels, target audience, competition, tone, etc.

But our *answer* to 'What is the campaign's desired impact?' (i.e., What do we want the audience to think, feel, and do after viewing our message) was *one* word: 'Goose bumps'.

I am pleased to say that Travis and the team delivered. I will soon share the campaign video, hoping that it gives you 'goose bumps' too – if not, check for a pulse.

What tickles me, and I wonder, 'Do goose bumps (emotion) change perceptions?'

Like most people, I too get goose bumps, *when*:

- I see an emotional ending to a movie with crescendoing music.
- I see sparkles in my kids' eyes when they achieve something significant – score a goal, get straight *A*s, or discover something new.
- Someone talks passionately about their work.
- I see someone doing something *good* to others, from their heart.

What gives you goose bumps?

Post # 138

Gotta love millennials

#Thisiswhatticklesme

Forgive me for being a little provocative, with a sprinkle of tough love. Gotta love millennials.

They want to change the world and be millionaires, armed with their knowledge of essential oils.

Is the song – *Gotta Love Millennials* – a little harsh? Maybe, but there is no smoke without fire.

I've written about this before, but this song tickled me to write again, because I care and because they will soon run the world and look after me when I am old.

Millennials' top five important factors for finding a job has nothing to do with the actual job.

They want a sense of meaning, flexible working hours, the opportunity to be a leader, work/life balance, and getting a chance to go to professional training programmes.

#Thisiswhatticklesme

Do I sense a little 'entitlement' here?

Maybe they just need some love.

If they want to sit on the beach counting fluffy clouds, posting pictures, and looking for meaning in life, because that's what makes them happy, I'd say *do it.*

But they can't expect a medal for participating or the next promotion.

I say to millennials, 'I love you; you are our future. Don't be needy; you are entitled to nothing you don't deserve. Work *hard*, be passionate, and you shall receive.'

Your views?

Post # 139

Look, Ma, I am eating my veggies!

#Thisiswhatticklesme

I felt like I didn't belong. I felt like I was from another planet. I have witnessed it before and have been forced into it a couple of times.

But this time, I took special notice of a group of 20-somethings, in a restaurant.

I was very intrigued by the meticulous process, the pauses, the angles, the fake smiles during the 'shoot', and the look of indifference before and after.

Then comes the post 'shoot' review of each picture. The pictures must be approved before and after the filters and certainly before they are posted.

This process has been mastered by females; males do it too, but they are amateurs at it.

Yes, I am talking about this crazy phenomenon called the 'selfie'.

To a certain degree, I can understand that when friends get together, it's OK to take a couple of pictures for the record, the albums, or to let Travis know that they met without him.

But I can't understand why this continues for most of the evening. How many do they need?

Now, what tickles me is when they start taking pictures of their food!

Really! Why?

If it is for health reasons and they are sending it to their mother for her approval, then I can understand.

But who wants to see what you are having for dinner?

Please help me understand.

Post # 140

Pssst, come here . . . 90 per cent discount!

#Thisiswhatticklesme

It's that time again . . . 'The lull before the storm'. The storm of going back to school, an overdose of meetings and activities, and the avalanche of conferences and trade shows.

Come mid-September, 'All hell breaks loose'.

But in the meantime, we have the usual consumer retail–therapy activities in stores.

- Buy 1, get 1 free
- 30 per cent cashback (really a 30 per cent discount – sometimes against your next purchase)
- 90 per cent off with some twist or another

What tickles me is that we, the consumers, are suckers for these promotions. Some of us just love them.

#Thisiswhatticklesme

I rarely buy at full price. Why?

Because retailers treat us as dumbo consumers! They are telling us that we are ripping you off the rest of the year, but we are going to be fair, honest, and feel sorry for you four or five times a year. The rest of the year, only the desperate and those who like to burn holes in their pockets are welcome.

Fact: Retailers sell 50 per cent more during the promotion period.

Why not just have 'everyday low prices' and sell more!

Nooooo, that's not exciting enough for us shoppers. We love to see big signs and before and after prices! Even if the 'before' price is inflated.

I propose a more honest approach:

- Inflated price season
- Reasonable price season

Are you a sale or a regular-price shopper?

Post # 141

Think 'jugaad'

#Thisiswhatticklesme

Every time I visit this fascinating city: 'Lahore – Lahore Hai', I am always tickled and amazed by the 'can do' attitude I find here.

They have an awesome word: 'jugaad', which means 'It will be done, whichever way!'

I saw Awais adamant to get not one but two glass panels fixed pronto. He asked his buddy Babar to get him to his destination on his modest motorcycle.

#Thisiswhatticklesme

Obviously, this is not the safest way to transport glass! But Awais didn't care.

Need to remind myself of that 'jugaad' attitude, but I would certainly use a slightly safer method.

Be like Awais (minus the risk); think 'jugaad'.

Post # 142

Murphy's law

#Thisiswhatticklesme

We've been to the moon and back and conquered outer space, yet no presentation or conference goes without a technical glitch.

Murphy's law!
    'Anything that can go wrong will go wrong.'

What tickles me is that no matter how much you prepare, test, retest, and rehearse your presentation, the probability of something going wrong on your big day is as certain as death and taxes.

I was recently at a marketing conference, where I was speaking – I did everything possible to ensure a smooth flow. I tested the sound, played the videos, briefed the team when to dim the lights, etc.

The minute I started my presentation, the clicker didn't work, the video played with no sound, and then the presentation froze!

#Thisiswhatticklesme

But then I found that my glitches were a walk in the park compared to what happened to other presenters:

The audio/visual team put the wrong presentation, videos played in slow motion, and then the computer crashed.

The worst part is when everything stops and you are standing in front of hundreds of people staring at you.

So, I now prepare a couple of jokes.

- Communism jokes aren't funny unless everyone gets them.
- One cow to the other, 'You ever worry about mad cow disease?' The other cow says, 'Why would I care? I'm a helicopter.'

Have you encountered Murphy's law?

Post # 143

Psychoanalyse this!

#Thisiswhatticklesme

People psychoanalyse people, and companies psychoanalyse people all the time. There is a lot of psychoanalysis going on.

Some use personal judgement, and some use of proven methods and tools.

What tickles me is that I have done them all. I have been colour-coded and labelled everything in the book. They put me in boxes and gave me strange acronyms like ENTJ.

We are also psychoanalysing brands and categories by their colour.

Below are highlights from an article written by a splendid agency called Coley Porter Bell (I worked with them on a global rebranding project) about colour and product labels:

- People make a subconscious judgement about a product or person within 90 seconds of their initial interaction, and 62–90 per cent of that assessment is based on colour alone.
- Blue and white communicate a sense of cleanliness, freshness, and efficacy.
- Red evokes urgency/power and demands attention.
- In sensitive skincare, green rules.
- In fast food, red and yellow dominate – they evoke speed or a sense of urgency.

If you psychoanalyse me: I am a *red* brand sprinkled with a rainbow.

Who are you?

Post # 144

Naked on board – for your safety

#Thisiswhatticklesme

Naughty, naughty, instead of tuning in, I get tickled, and I tune out!

That's what happens when the safety video comes on and the flight attendants 'hit the stage and start doing strange hand signals' before every takeoff!!

The instructions are the same every time . . . but some airlines have made it super entertaining using celebrities, comedians, and even *naked* flight attendants to get our attention.

- Fasten your seat belt – like this

Yawn!

- Don't hit your fellow passenger with your over-sized bag

- Remove your fancy designer shoes (eeeww!) before you jump on the bouncy castle
- Put the oxygen mask on first, before helping Travis
- Don't smoke, and if you do, we'll fine you US$2K

And on some airlines

- Don't argue with flight attendants, or they'll beat the sh$t out of you and drag your bottom off the plane

You know what I mean!

But why do they do that on each and every flight?

This is done to remind us and to 'rewire' our brain in case of an accident.

That's why in business we do crisis and other trainings for managers on a regular basis to remind them of procedures and instructions 'like' putting the oxygen mask on first, before helping Travis.

Do you 'tune in', or do you count sheep?

Post # 145

Turkish cay and simit . . . Forget afternoon tea

#Thisiswhatticklesme

I can't come to Turkey TR and not have tea (çay) and simit – my favourite breakfast.

I developed this habit when I lived in beautiful Istanbul – you can easily have five to six cups of tea per day, summer or winter, rain or sunshine.

My diet in Turkey involved tea . . .

Before, during, and after breakfast.
Several times at work.
At every meeting.
Before, during, and after lunch.

You get the picture . . .

So, forget about 'afternoon tea'! It's an all-day affair.

#Thisiswhatticklesme

Turkey is, by far, the biggest per capita consumer of tea in the world.

I can't imagine Turkey without it.

You would think it's part of the constitution!

One would think that tea is part of Turkey's heritage and history, but that's not true . . .

What tickled me is that despite its popularity, tea only became the beverage of choice in TR in the early 1900s. It was initially encouraged as an alternative to coffee, which had become expensive and at times unavailable after World War I.

I was also happy to learn that tea is actually good for you, as it contains antioxidants, less caffeine than coffee, and may help with weight loss (that's *not* working for me)!

Just a tickling thought: What do you think would happen if they ban tea in Turkey?

Post # 146

I quit

#Thisiswhatticklesme

'I *quit*' – two impactful words any person can say or do in their professional life. They often have a common cause.

People *don't* resign because:

- The internet speed is not fast enough (to view vacation videos on FB).
- Their parking spot is too far from the entrance.
- They don't have an espresso machine on their floor.
- The food in the canteen is not organic.

What tickles me is that some people still don't realise that:

People don't leave companies; they leave managers.

Again, people don't leave companies they work for; they leave bad managers they work with.

#Thisiswhatticklesme

Bad managers are the primary reason (more than 50 per cent) why people resign from their jobs.

Managers can make or break your career, and they have a huge impact on your motivation.
(70 per cent of the factors that contribute to happiness at work are directly related to managers.)

The cost of bad managers is too high to tolerate – losing talent costs money.

I have been fortunate to work for three companies in my professional life.

I guess I have been lucky to have quality managers. (Boss(es), please take note.)
Note to quality managers: Be a leader; empower your people, and be fair.

Note to bad managers: What goes around, comes around.

Post # 147

I am cool again!

#Thisiswhatticklesme

'I want a polaroid camera for my birthday,' my daughter demanded.

'Really! How do you even know about that old clunky camera?' I asked.

'It's *cool*!' she said.

I showed her a picture of me playing an ancient pinball machine, with a 'real' ball.

'*Wow*, that's crazy, crazy,' she said.

I used to play pinball for hours at the neighbourhood game centre with friends physically there, cheering me on.

Retro is back?

- Polaroid cameras and expensive film cartridges are back.
- Turntables and vinyl records are back.
- Typewriters are back, really?
- Pinball machines will be back! I hope.

#Thisiswhatticklesme

I demand that it becomes an Olympic sport.

What is going on and why?
It's tickling, and I wonder:*When will these be back*?

- Calling the bank and speaking to a real person vs pressing 27 buttons first.
- Going to a café, where people actually talk to each other vs stare at screens.
- Meet a person and not have to take a selfie.
- Wait 24 hours to develop my pictures – hoping the guy at the film shop doesn't judge me based on my pictures.

Soon these retro ideas will become a differentiating factor for brands and businesses – the wave has started.

What else do you hope comes back?

Regardless, all that matters is that I am *cool* again.

Post # 148

What does your modern press release look like?

#Thisiswhatticklesme

Is my important press release going in your vertical filing (a.k.a. shredder)?

Unless it's paid or you like me or you're hoping for some ads or because it's genuinely newsworthy.

This has been tickling me for a while.

I remember back in the days when we worked hard to put together a wordy jargon-filled press release with a quote or two and a printed photo with a caption on the back.

Then Travis, from our PR agency, got on his moped and physically delivered it to publications.

Fast-forward to 2017.

We still do that!

Except Travis lost his job to e-mail/PDF/jpg files.

We still send lengthy jargon-filled press releases with a 'tickling' quote, because no one actually speaks like these quotes.

Attach a file/link to download a logo and picture, and if we are going all out, include an mpeg file (video).

So, we haven't really moved on; or have we?

Surely a PR campaign is a lot more than a press release, but this item is still included in the deliverables and in the old format + its measurability is a dog's dinner.

(Exaggerating to make a point.)

Should brands create newsworthy, relevant, and entertaining content in the form of 'posts', publications/influencers would just package and share or print it.

What does your modern press release look like?

Post # 149

You called me for this?

#Thisiswhatticklesme

'You called me for *this*?' said my teenage son!

'Yes, I called to check on you and see if you are still alive,' was my response.

The rest below were said by 'Travis':

- 'If it's a phone call, then it must be serious.'
- 'If he wanted to chat, he should text me.'
- 'If it's not urgent, we can just do it on WhatsApp.'
- 'What do you mean you don't have WhatsApp?'

I 'hear' this all the time now. Humans don't like calls anymore.

They hate it . . . they feel calls are intrusive.

Humans now use text to wish other humans 'Happy Birthday'; give 'condolences'; and when they are sick, to wish them well.

#Thisiswhatticklesme

And we have emojis for each one.

Humans much prefer to text even for business, customer service, etc. . . . and companies are responding.

This is applicable to all ages now, but surely much more to the younger generation.

Should we start calling these devices 'living devices' vs 'smartphones', because the 'phone' feature is now secondary and without them we can't 'live' anymore?

What tickles me most is not what's happening now but where we will be in 20 years.

Will the phone join the telex and the fax to the grave?

Any futurists amongst us?

Post # 150

Would you hire this guy?

#Thisiswhatticklesme

I was offered a job today; not my dream job, but a job nonetheless.

I was talking to my daughter Sam – who is studying to be a doctor – about life, starting a career, and getting a job.

You know, the heart-to-heart type.

She said, 'But, Dad, it's hard!'

To encourage her, I said, 'Sam, it's all about passion and the right attitude.'

A couple of hours later, we went shopping at the local supermarket and saw this 'Now Hiring' sign!

#Thisiswhatticklesme

I said to Sam, 'Let me demonstrate how to get a job.'

I asked for the manager in a determined and confident way!

Sam was standing about 'a mile' away from me thinking, 'I don't know him.'

I went up to the store manager with a big, serious smile; showed her the photo, and said, 'I know this guy; he is a burst of energy, knows retail inside out, and he is obsessed with food! Would you hire him?'

Pause . . . she took a second look at the photo and then at me!

'With that attitude, you're hired. When can you start?' she said with a happy smile.

Sam emerged from behind the cereal aisle, where she was hiding, rolled her eyes, and said, 'OK, OK, got it, now let's go home . . . enough embarrassment!'

I thought so too!

Post # 151

I trust you . . . I don't trust you

#Thisiswhatticklesme

'I don't trust you,' said no one ever to motivate or encourage someone.

It all started back in my high school days when I was in boarding school.

The frightening headmaster (let's call him 'Travis') called me into his office; he had a telex sheet in his hand and a faint smirk on his face.

Yes, those days we communicated via telex.

The telex was from my father, granting me permission to do whatever I wanted during weekends, because 'he trusts his son'.

#Thisiswhatticklesme

'I don't usually get these types of messages; you realise the responsibility this puts on you,' headmaster Travis said.

The fact that I was allowed to do whatever I wanted (nothing was 'forbidden') made me less likely to 'get into trouble' and do silly things.

In other words, I was a good boy!

I didn't realise how profound this message was to me! Then and now . . .

Today, when I meet someone (friend or colleague), I usually, though not all the time, start with a *full* 'tank' of trust – giving them my full trust from the beginning.

Vs

An *empty* one, where it's up to them to earn it.

It works for me and makes me less anxious, less of a micro manager, and hopefully motivates them.

What's your formula?

Are you a *full* or an *empty* tanker?

Post # 152

For every action, there is . . .

#Thisiswhatticklesme

I was cycling on a Sunday afternoon in a small picturesque town called 'Niagara-on-the-Lake'.

I was pleasantly shocked. The first time I crossed a cyclist, he and everyone in his group said, 'Hi' or 'Hello'.

I thought, 'Do I know them from somewhere? I don't remember. Have I lost my mind?'

The next group of cyclists and the next, all greeted me with a friendly 'Hello' and a gentle nod as if we were long-lost friends.

I couldn't believe it.

Then I tried it.

Everyone I crossed along the way, I initiated the 'Hello' gesture, and I got an eager, bright, and friendly 'Hello' back, with a smile.

#Thisiswhatticklesme

'Hey, these people are friendly,' I thought. What a friendly and welcoming environment.

But then I remembered my physics class . . .

'For every action, there is an equal and opposite reaction.'

It tickles me that we don't do enough of that at work. All it takes is a small effort to salute our colleagues, even if we don't 'know' them.

Imagine the atmosphere around the office . . .

Instead of the grumpy or sometimes hurried 'I am too busy' look with a mumbled 'Morning' . . .

What happened to the full sentence?

'Good morning'.

Small things . . .

I am not your mushy or bubbly type, but I am reminded that 'kindness' is easily reciprocated and goes a *long* way, regardless of race, colour, or religion.

Post # 153

Happy Birthday to 7 billion people!

#Thisiswhatticklesme

Today (13 August) is the day I was born into this marvellous world.

We were all born! That's swell!

So why is today special? Why is my birthday special? Why is your birthday special?

I am so tickled by this whole birthday thingymajiggy.

On our birthday, people wish us 'Happy Birthday'.

I wonder why they do that.

What is so happy about it? *Why* is it different from any other day?

If I am generally happy, will I be happier on my birthday?

#Thisiswhatticklesme

Is it because we are celebrating that we haven't been hit by a bus and that we are still alive?

Are your friends, family, and colleagues so happy that you were born? Are they really?

Or is it because we feel loved and important, or because we receive so many gifts, likes, posts, and WhatsApp messages?

Why not ask the UN to designate a global Birth Day, just like:

World Milk Day, World Yoga Day, World Mental Health Day, World Tourism Day, World Tuna Day, World Poetry Day . . . many world days, but *no* World Birth Day!

So much waste! We do that over seven billion times every year!

If we concentrate the celebration to one day . . . we would save on mushy birthday cards, the annoying birthday messages, and the impersonal birthday e-mails.

But until then, I intend to celebrate my birthday in style!

Happy Birthday to me.

Post # 154

Is that a job title?

#Thisiswhatticklesme

Sitting at a bar, waiting for a friend to arrive . . .
A young (in his early 20s), sleek, and confident guy comes and sits next to me.

Let's call him 'Travis'.

Within 30 seconds, he hit me with a 'Wassup!'

He talked too much, but I finally managed to ask a question. 'So, what do you do?'

'I am an insta influencer', he said.

'Is that a real job title? Are you like an employee in a company?' I asked.

'Yup' – he said – 'only it's mine.'

Here is what I learnt from Travis about influencers:

- They are like a TV station, only with fewer overheads.
- They are authentic/real/unfiltered.
- They impact purchase decisions.
- They achieve high engagement (real e.g.: Brand X averaged 2K engagements in June on its owned posts, while influencer posts had an average of 240K engagements – that is more than 100 times the engagement level from the brand's own posts).
- Top influencers are often paid more than US$100K for a single mention.
- The tricky part is matching influencers and companies. This applies to B2C and B2B companies.
- B2C is a 'walk in the park' compared to B2B.
- A common mistake for B2B companies is that they keep their messages wordy, jargony, and not relevant to the goldfish attention-span swipers.

Note to self: When I grow up, I wanna be an insta influencer, *just* like Travis.

Post # 155

My Zen Zone

#Thisiswhatticklesme

I am not into yoga, nor am I into the spiritual hallelujah 'stuff'.

But the more I know about this 'stuff', the more I learn to respect them, what they stand for, and what they can do for you – it tickles me.

I now take a couple of moments a day to go into the 'Zen Zone', a.k.a. 'ZZ' . . .
    (Not sure how long this will last, but I am giving it a shot.)

In short, it's all about focus! It is about mindfulness (new buzz word).

Focus on positive things, being fully present in a relaxed mode, and not worrying about things that you cannot change.

Cool as a cucumber . . .

#Thisiswhatticklesme

Zen was originally developed in Japan, and it emphasises that knowledge is achieved through emptying the mind of thoughts and giving attention to only one thing.

Not a religion. It is a state of mind.

Zen things to do:

- Think positively and occasionally smile
- Do one thing at a time, deliberately and completely
- Do less, and live simply

In conclusion: If you wake up in the morning and think about miserable things, you'll have a miserable day.

If you wake up and focus instead on positive things, you'll have a splendid day.

DND – time for my 'ZZ' moment now . . .

Post # 156

Silk, silk, silk . . .

#Thisiswhatticklesme

Repeat after me . . . silk, silk, silk, silk, silk . . .
What do cows drink?
. . .
Ha, ha, ha, admit it, you said or thought 'milk'.

No, cows don't drink milk; they drink water.

That is the power of brain conditioning, shortcuts, and familiarity.

The above is a crude but powerful example of how the brain works.

Social scientists have studied implicit stereotypes of race, sex, and other attributes based on these patterns of mental connections. And linguists have looked at how our brains organise and access words by testing which words are more associated with each other.

#Thisiswhatticklesme

This is what we do in marketing and communications every day, sometimes without knowing it.

We condition consumers' brains with what we show and tell them, and what we repeat.

Don't get bored with your message, repeat it again and again, and it will eventually register.

Winston Churchill once said, 'If you have an important point to make, don't try to be subtle or clever. Use a pile driver. Hit the point once. Then come back and hit it again. Then hit it a third time – a tremendous whack.'

Now! Seriously?
We don't water cows; we milk them.
So where is this US$2.19 water from?

Post # 157

Falafel – lobster, same, same, but different

#Thisiswhatticklesme

When in Rome . . . that's what I have been doing here in Prince Edward Island . . . lobster for breakfast, lunch, and dinner.

Lobster in salad, lobster burgers, lobster-designed napkins and posters, lobster coming out of my ears!

It's less expensive than a falafel sandwich in Dubai.

Does the old theory of supply and demand apply?

Or is it positioning?

I was tickled to learn that lobster was a poor man's food in the 18th century. There was so much of it that people started serving lobsters to their pigs, cows, and cats, while Native Americans used them as fertiliser and fish bait.

But then positioning kicked in!

In the late 1800s, some genius marketers (railway managers) discovered that if they billed it as a delicacy, passengers who didn't know of its disgusting reputation would think it was delicious.

By the 1920s, it had become the food of choice for the world's aristocrats.

Now, can we find a marketing genius to position Dom Pérignon as a poor man's drink for a week?

Post # 158

'I agree with everything you say! But it be just your eyes . . . xx' –Uncool

#Thisiswhatticklesme

I am not an activist. I like to think of myself as a decent guy with common sense!

Which is not that common these days.

I come across many posts, and many are awesome, but some tickle me!

Recently, a young, ambitious, and accomplished lady posted something about an event she was speaking at in LA . . .

She was proud of herself and her upcoming opportunity to speak about something important ('The Art of Giving and Taking'), and some of the comments on her post were simply rubbish!

#Thisiswhatticklesme

That's not right!

No one asks me for my phone number or compliments my eyes!

Why not?

On a serious note!

Guys, you know who you are! Grow up, and stop it!

There are many shady places where you can use these pickup lines, just not here.

Post # 159

Guilty!

#Thisiswhatticklesme

Guilty until proven innocent! That's how every traveller is presumed, including me. What happened to trust?

Today I passed through airport security, and I was a little tickled.

'We don't trust you, so we are going to search you; scan you; and in some cases, strip you' – that is what airport security all over the world is telling you.

Remove your laptop, iPad, watch, belt, shoes, jacket, and put all your liquids in some little measly plastic bag!

Do they have a good reason? Maybe, but sometimes they can be a little ridiculous.

You can't even take a water bottle onboard! Seriously? Any liquid above 100 ml is dangerous. Is it?

#Thisiswhatticklesme

My perfume bottle is a potential detonating device! I can't even utter the *B* word.

Sadly, one lunatic here and another lunatic there, and now we *all* have to be treated like criminals.

Looking at the bright side, I do enjoy the thorough 'pat down' service that I get every time I travel.

Some guys take their job seriously, and I like it because I get a free massage every time (maybe because of the titanium I have in my leg).

Post # 160

Nothing is good

#Thisiswhatticklesme

Once or twice a year, when I am on vacation, I go into a 'nothing' mode. I switch off and I:

- Do nothing
- Plan nothing
- Think nothing

'Nothing' is not bad. It clears your mind. It's a detox for your brain.

'Nothing' is defined as:

- Something that does not exist
- The absence of all magnitude or quantity
- A vacuum – space void of matter
- The concept denoting the absence of something

What tickles me is that so many good, big, existential ideas and thoughts come to me when I am in my 'nothing' mode.

#Thisiswhatticklesme

So 'nothing' is good.

And I mean it in a 'good' way.

But then I learnt that there is something called the study of 'nothing'.

So 'nothing' is actually a serious something.

If you talk to a physicist, you may get a different answer. According to quantum physics, even vacuums are not completely empty.

I have 'nothing' meaningful to add.

Post # 161

'Yalla, when are you coming home? Bring milk.'

#Thisiswhatticklesme

I remember that day vividly, in Montréal, 28 years ago. I was fortunate to be given a mobile phone.

I was so excited.

It was to me what an iPhone 15 would be to Generation Z.

I would call my brother at home and ask him to call me on my mobile phone, so I could pull it out of my back pocket in front of my friends.

It was for showing off really, as I didn't have anyone to call.

Sadly, the conversation was limited to a 'Bonjour, kefak, ça va?' or the occasional 'Yalla, when are you coming home? Bring milk.'

The 'phone' was used purely for 'phone calls' . . . get it? Phone – phone calls!

No text, no Emojis, no apps, no GPS, and no LinkedIn.

The world has moved on in 30 odd years, and now we call them 'smartphones'!

In comparison to what I had, yes, these new gadgets are bloody smart. They do everything for you!

Smartphones now still let you communicate (thankfully), find your long-lost friend, book a dentist appointment or a vacation, order a pizza, and could potentially sort out your lousy love life.

I wonder what phones would look like or do in 2030 . . .

Post # 162

Sophie, make me handsome again!

#Thisiswhatticklesme

I thought I was unique and special. Nonsense!
 Robots are an eye blink away from conquering our world, and there will be another me.

Today, automation and technology enable us to have self-driving cars, trains, and auto-piloted planes, play music, run factories, analyse complex algorithms, and much more.

But all these machines run under our command! We control them. We tell them when to start, when to stop, and what to do. Not anymore!

Robots, like Sophie, have come a long way! They have an attitude, a sense of humour, and some have even invented their own code language (not English) to communicate efficiently with each other.

#Thisiswhatticklesme

Reminds me of the series *Westworld* . . .

My prediction for the future!

I predict that each of us will have a clone robot that will be with us from the day we are born – programmed with our emotions and personality, a robot that represents us in real life.

The real person will sit on the beach and contemplate life, and their robot replica will be at work making $$$.

I also suspect that robots will soon be able to do miracles.

'Sophie, make me handsome again!'

Post # 163

What the hell was I thinking?

#Thisiswhatticklesme

This month, 25 years ago, I started in advertising. I was young, hungry, and dumb.

During my university years, marketing and advertising were the only classes I would stay awake in, mesmerised by how it all worked.

I started my first real job in an industry I was fascinated by throughout my youth. It was cool, it was sexy, it was like *Mad Men*.

What the hell was I thinking?

I would stop at, look at, and read every advert (a walking sponge); I loved creativity. (Still do.)

#Thisiswhatticklesme

What tickled me the most is the power of the advert to influence people to think, feel, and do something that they wouldn't otherwise.

You were the doctor here to help! You were respected, and you worked your butt off.

Looking back, everything was manual, everything was done from scratch, and every ad was built by hand, like a Rolls Royce.

It was magical!

Things have changed since; it's so much faster. There is an app for almost everything; content creators (Spielbergs) are a dime a dozen, and everyone is an adman/woman.

Advertising is now measured by likes, views, and going viral . . . and going viral means you have to do something nuts, controversial, or a 'social experiment'.

But creativity remains scarce – bring it back . . . please.

Post # 164

Nearly all men can stand adversity, but if you want to test a man's character, give him power

—Abraham Lincoln

#Thisiswhatticklesme

I don't usually like to drop names! But this quote, by this historical man, tickled me. For me, to really test a man's character, give him money, on top of power.

I have seen people, let's call them 'Bob', once in a high-power position with a sprinkle of money, transform into ugly monsters . . .

A couple of years before it all got to their head, they were a timid and lost puppy.

Others, let's call them 'Jim', have become more gracious with others and generous with their time and money.

#Thisiswhatticklesme

Jim sometimes even visits his old neighbourhood where he grew up, to meet old friends, to remind himself of where he came from, and to make him more appreciative of what he has.

No matter how far or how high you go,

Don't be a Bob; be a Jim.

Post # 165

Can 145 elephants fly?

#Thisiswhatticklesme

I am always tickled and in awe at how science and technology work.

I still can't come to terms with the idea that a 'city' of 600+ people (a.k.a. Airbus A380) with all their belongings and junk can defy gravity and fly.

This bird has a max takeoff weight capacity of 575 tons . . . that's approximately 145 elephants . . . isn't that splendid?

And today I learnt that NASA is developing ways to grow vegetables in space! Mars, to be specific. Kudos!

This is where technology has brought us, and some people still complain about trivial things like:

- My coffee is not hot enough.
- My raisin bran had too many raisins in it this morning.

#Thisiswhatticklesme

- My mobile is dying . . . but my charger is all the way upstairs.
- What do you mean, 'No Wi-Fi'?
- I don't have enough likes.

Ok, end of rant.

Post # 166

Believe me, I am attractive

#Thisiswhatticklesme

'No, I want that table by the window!' said the tall, well-dressed, and attractive woman, with an attitude.

'Of course!' said the maître d' without hesitation.

Ten mins earlier that same table was supposedly 'reserved', when a less attractive person asked, who was then led to a table by the kitchen door. This tickled me – I have witnessed similar situations before but didn't pause to think as much. A person on my table said, 'Well, attractive people get their way!'

It reminded me of a 2011 book, *Beauty Pays: Why Attractive People Are More Successful*, by Daniel Hamermesh, an economist at the University of Texas. His research (and several others') showed that attractive people:

- Both men and women, earn an average of 3–4 per cent more than people with below-average looks, over a lifetime.

- Are hired sooner, get promotions more quickly, and are higher ranking in their companies.
- Often bring more money to their companies and therefore are more valuable employees.
- Are more likely to obtain bank loans and pay lower interest rates than below-average-looking borrowers – same demographic, age, gender, and credit history.

That explains why I have to constantly fight with my bank to offer me lower interest rates.

I know looks matter and being presentable matters – but this much?

Thoughts!

Post # 167

Sam, got time for a pina colada?

#Thisiswhatticklesme

Sam's hotshot lawyer job is on the line!

Machines replaced assembly-line jobs, automation and AI will soon replace bank-tellers' jobs, but I didn't see this one coming.

Sam, my lawyer, will soon have more time on the beach sipping pina coladas.

Because 'Smart Contract', which is run by Ethereum blockchain, could soon replace lawyers.

Ethereum is a decentralised blockchain platform that will execute as programmed (*If* this happens, *then* do that triggers) without any possibility of downtime, fraud, or third-party interference.

#Thisiswhatticklesme

Example:

I am renting my house to Tom for US$25K/year from 01.01.2019; we can now do this through the blockchain by paying in cryptocurrency.

Tom gets a receipt that is held in our virtual contract, with agreed terms, like ($200/day surcharge after 31.12.19).

So, *if* Tom returns the e-keys on 31.12.2019, *then* I get paid US$25k.

If not and he returns them on 10.01.2020, *then* his account is debited an additional US$2k.

No negotiations, no give me a discount, habibi. All this is 'witnessed' by hundreds of people online.

NOTE: No mediator making money or enforcing the contract. No lawyers, no Airbnb, no Visa or MasterCard.

Just me and Tom.

So, Sam, got time for a pina colada?

Basic 'Smart Contract' code here.

Post # 168

#Thisiswhatticklesme

Imagine you are Ms./Mr. Blue shirt (in the picture above), and you are happily working at a company that sells coconut water with Mr. Red and Ms./Mr. Purple shirts!

Both are nice people; they are committed, hardworking, and can be annoying at times, like most colleagues.

You worked your behind off to be able to reach your position and now sit in the corner office of Coconut Land Co.,

#Thisiswhatticklesme

have seniority benefits, and four weeks' vacation. (You think you've earned your stool.)

One fine day, your boss tells you that to be *equitable* in this company . . . you'll have to give up the corner office, some of your perks, and reduce your vacation to two and a half weeks, so Ms./Mr. Purple shirt (a newcomer) can have the same benefits, and Coconut Land Co. could keep costs the same.

But you'll still have a job. How would you feel?

Are you for Equality or Equity?

Easy choice?

PS.
Equality is giving everyone a shoe.
Equity is giving everyone a shoe that fits.

Image source: IISC

Post # 169

Girl power!

#Thisiswhatticklesme

A hard-headed and opinionated colleague, whom I happen to respect, was talking to me about 'diversity at work'.

She said, 'The diversity on my team is great!'

'Who do you have on your team?' I asked.

She said, 'Eight lovely and smart ladies'.

'Is this your definition of diversity?' I asked.

I reminded her that gender diversity is defined as 'equitable ratio between men and women'.

She smirked and walked away.

I support any kind of diversity, but it should be based on merit and competence, regardless.

#Thisiswhatticklesme

I don't subscribe to giving any man or woman a job to meet some diversity quota, but because of his/her qualifications and experience.

I believe, from experience and based on research of over a million people, that women can have a 'brighter bulb' than men.

Women are better at relationship management, have higher EQ (90 per cent of top performers are high in EQ), and deliver better-quality work – when they want to.

I also believe that my daughter, who is now a beautiful 20-year-old, will be the best doctor in the world!

Am I biased? Yes.
Is she worthy of my belief? You bet!

All the *power* to her . . .

Post # 170

Am I OCD or just a tidy civilian?

#Thisiswhatticklesme

A dear friend gets a kick out of my obsession with tidiness and cleanliness.

Every time he comes over for a beverage, he would deliberately leave a trail of crumbs or pistachio shells on the counter and wait for me to instantly pick them up midconversation. It amuses him what I would do unconsciously. I can't see something out of place and just leave it there! I can't.

Don't judge me.

People are usually judged by their general appearance, their shoes (*Oh boy*, do shoes matter!), and their smile/teeth.

For me, ditto above, but I usually notice how clean the inside of their car is and how tidy their desk is.

#Thisiswhatticklesme

I have seen car interiors that look like they've been hit by a hurricane . . . or what I would call a mobile garbage bin.

Also, having a tidy and organised desk tells me a lot about the individual's personality – clear, uncluttered, organised, focused?

Thankfully we have a CDP (Clean Desk Policy) in our company, which requires employees to leave their desk clean and clear of all papers or junk when they leave the office.

Am I OCD or just a tidy civilian?

Post # 171

PS. I wasn't flirting

#Thisiswhatticklesme

A smile is contagious; try it!
　　Last weekend, I was out with a couple of friends (yes, I have friends) at a casual restaurant.

We had a rude and grumpy waitress serving us. She was disinterested and hurried us with our order.

I was tickled, to say the least, but I had taken a 'chill' pill earlier that evening, so I decided to change things.

When my turn came to give my order, I said with a big smile:
　　'I would like a burger made with *love* and a *smile*, please.'

She paused, tilted her head, and looked at me . . . I repeated my order.

She smiled!

I said, 'You look so much prettier with a smile, and . . . I am *not* flirting with you.'

I got a bigger smile; she changed completely, and the evening turned out marvellous.

In the end, she got a nice tip with a big smiley drawn on the bill.

So many benefits to smiling:
Endorphins, released when you smile, are responsible for lowering stress levels.

- Smiling acts as the body's natural painkiller.
- Smiling makes you more attractive to others.
- It takes 17 muscles to smile and 42 muscles to frown.

Conclusion: Flex *only* 17 facial muscles – it's free, good for your health and your business, and makes you look good!

Post # 172

I can't show off anymore!

#Thisiswhatticklesme

On a recent trip to Sweden, where I frequent for work, I tried to do the unthinkable.

One fine Swedish summer day, the fluffy cotton clouds were arrogantly covering the sun – like the tropics, it rained every hour on the hour. It was a chilly 18°C, like a Dubai conference room, and I wanted to buy a cup of coffee to warm up with.

I walked into a café and ordered my much-awaited cup of strong Swedish coffee – no competition with Turkish coffee, though.

When the bill came, I was asked,

'How would you like to pay?'

I said, 'I'll pay cash, as I have accumulated some Swedish kronas from previous visits.'

He said, 'OK, but we may not have enough change to pay you back, as we are a cashless café.'

On reflection and after extensive research on Google (3 min), I learnt that *only* 3 per cent of Sweden's economy is cash!

The cashless society thing is actually happening. Yet another thing that technology is disruptively changing.

I remember the days when I used to show off my wallet to my friends, full of foreign currency notes – look, how many countries I've been to!

Sadly, I can no longer do that, as I can now travel to a dozen countries without the need or hassle of exchanging money or using ATM machines.

I now have an app to show off with!

Post # 173

Martial arts studio

#Thisiswhatticklesme

You have a nice and uneventful flight.
    You watch a movie, which you miss half of because you fall asleep several times.

You try to eat a meal without painting your shirt the same colour as your food.

You do some work on your computer, if you can open your laptop. (The guy in front of you decides to recline his seat throughout the flight.)

Yes, I am referring to economy class!
Business-class passengers don't know what I am talking about – you might as well stop reading.

You arrive in one piece, and the plane reaches the gate.

That's when you get an instant martial arts studio onboard!

#Thisiswhatticklesme

The nice old lady who was sitting next to you turns out to be a black belt in karate, and the charming man sitting across the aisle is actually a ninja in disguise – both eager to disembark (along with another 100+ passengers) when there is nowhere to go.

There's got to be a better way for airlines to manage the martial artists in us.

Post # 174

Don't be shy like a three-year-old!

#Thisiswhatticklesme

You are sitting in a meeting with colleagues, and the pressure is *on* to make an impression.

The presenter is trying to impress you by spewing some big and made-up words/terms.

You are sitting there anxious, and feeling that you're not the brightest bulb in the room, because you don't understand what the presenter is saying.

You ask the person to your left, 'What does he mean by "smart sales"?' She looks at you like a deer caught in a headlight, and shrugs.

You pretend that all is under control, but then the presenter hits you again. You write 'Circular Economy?' on a notepad and pass it to the person to your right.

#Thisiswhatticklesme

He spends a couple of seconds writing something on your pad. You're thinking, 'S$&t he knows what he's talking about.'

He passes the notepad back to you, and you're 'phew' relieved because it says:
    'No clue, but I can't wait for lunch!'

I discovered that 93.75 per cent of the time when I don't understand something, chances are that 89.02 per cent of the audience doesn't either. (PS. The #% are made up, but I'd bet they are accurate to the nearest 0.07 per cent.)

Solution: Proudly and arrogantly ask the presenter about her fancy words or terms.

Don't be shy . . . like a three-year-old boy (or girl) . . . there are times when the presenter doesn't know either.

Post # 175

You know you've matured when . . .

#Thisiswhatticklesme

'I refuse to let anyone ruin my day.'
My motto in life.

Last week, I was driving on one of Dubai's busy and crazy roads.

The car in front of me abruptly and dangerously changed lanes twice, without using the turn signal. A normal occurrence, isn't it?

This time though I got tickled and flashed him with my high beam once, OK, maybe twice.

He got annoyed and started to make sudden breaks whilst making rude hand gestures.

I continued to be annoyed, and I flashed him once more. He decided to *stop* his car in front of mine, got out, and briskly walked towards me, whilst verbally abusing me.

At that moment, I decided to take control of my emotions... because my young and hot-blooded self would have wanted to get out and start a fistfight.

But my mature self got out of the car with a big smile on my face and walked towards this angry man. I put my hands on his shoulders slowly and leaned in and whispered:
 'I am going on a date tonight, and I don't want a black eye from you . . . *I am sorry*'; then I hugged him.

Silence . . . then his face broke into a big, genuine smile . . . and he hugged me back and said, 'You completely defused me.'

We went on our separate ways.

I smirked and thought to myself, '*It's not worth it . . .*'
What would you have done?

Post # 176

A what computer?

#Thisiswhatticklesme!

It tickles me because I wasn't half as smart as my 16-year-old son when I was his age.

A couple of days back, my son asked me – unusually nicely – for a new computer!

So, because he asked nicely and he did well in his exams, I hesitated, but agreed.
    'Let's go to the mall to buy you a computer,' I said.

He smirked and said, 'No, Dad, I will order the parts online and build one, because I need a high-powered gaming computer.'

'A what computer?' I asked, a little puzzled.

To cut a long story short, he ordered all the parts online . . . ouch, ouch $$$ . . . and built his own computer at home with his friend.

I was impressed – he built a computer – and a storm of questions swirled in my head:

- Where did he learn how to do this?
- What university will he go to?
- Will he go to a traditional university?
- What will he do when he grows up?
- Are we nurturing this generation properly with the existing and sometimes backwards education system?
- Will I retire early?

Disclaimer: My son is a geek, coder, coach, commentator, and a semi-professional League of Legends and Overwatch gamer – and soon will start making more money than me.

Post # 177

Why so DESPACITO?

#Thisiswhatticklesme

'Sorry for the late response' is the first sentence of an e-mail from someone I sent an important e-mail to *three weeks ago*.

It reminded me of the latest song that plays on the radio every 21 seconds and repeats . . . 'Despacito'.

I know that the title means '*slowly*', but that's it . . . I don't understand anything after that – not even Bieber does.

I understand that my friend took his sweet time to respond to my important e-mail, but I don't understand how he does it.

I don't understand how he, and others like him, think it's OK to sit on an e-mail for weeks.

- Has he lost the will to live?
- Am I not that important to him?
- Does he hate his job so much?

- Do e-mails hide in his inbox and reappear weeks later?

Enough with the sarcasm.

Responsiveness is good etiquette. It's that simple.

If this only happens internally, then you have some dirty laundry to clean and fix.

If this happens with your customers – you are doomed; try another career: go fishing.

I can't sit on an e-mail for more than three days. If I don't know the answer, or if I am not ready to answer, I send a reply acknowledging their e-mail, and ask for more time.

So why so 'Despacito'?

Post # 178

Do not send me generic e-cards!

#Thisiswhatticklesme

Do not send me generic seasonal e-cards . . .

This week I received over 100+ generic, dull, lookalike e-cards on e-mail from people and companies I know and from some I don't.

Sadly, many end up in my junk/clutter file, and I delete them without even seeing them. What a waste!

A lot of time, effort, and resources go into making these e-cards, but how effective are they?

Sure, e-cards are more environmentally friendly than the traditional physical cards, but when they are sent in a mass e-mail, they are as good as useless.

Personalised e-cards can certainly work and will be appreciated. Do they require more effort? *Yes*. Do they take time? *Yes*.

#Thisiswhatticklesme

By personalised e-cards, I don't mean:
'Dear Khaled, we think you are intelligent, awesome, and fun to work with . . .' – whilst that is true, it is just creepy.

Let me demonstrate an example:
'Dear Khaled, I take this special occasion to personally thank you and your team for your support/business, and I want you to know that we have particularly enjoyed working with you on . . . XYZ. I wish you continued success and look forward to working with you again.' (You get my drift . . .)

Do you share my view?

Eid Mubarak to all.

PS. This is applicable to all seasonal greeting e-cards.

A business opportunity . . . who is in?

Post # 179

BOGOF?

#Thisiswhatticklesme

I've stayed in more hotels than I care to count.

One thing that still tickles me is the hotel room *'mini bar'* concept, which hasn't evolved in years. Who buys anything from this stale and silly overpriced silent shop?
    I am either cheap, price sensitive, or a normal guy who doesn't like to be ripped off; I've rarely bought anything from the mini bar, except water – when I am super thirsty and the hotel is too profit hungry to offer complimentary water.

Do you buy anything from the 'mini bar'?

Business opportunity:
I would love to democratise the mini bar to the captive audience in the room. Make it attractive, relevant, and cost competitive so that it even competes with hypermarket prices.

#Thisiswhatticklesme

Volume, volume, volume . . . using marketing and sales techniques (e.g., BOGOF) and some big data info about each guest's profile and preferences, we'll make sure to stock up relevant goodies so that *every* hotel guest makes a substantial purchase in the convenience of their room.

Ask any hotel: How much do you make from your mini bar sales every year? 100?

Give me the mini bar in your hotel, and I will triple the revenue and give you 125!

Who is in?

PS. BOGOF is not a bad word.
Buy One, Get One Free

Post # 180

TOP GUN
Tom, where did you go?

#Thisiswhatticklesme

I observed that agencies will bring in their best, their 'Top Guns', the Tom Cruises, to the pitch.

What tickles me is that once they win the pitch, the 'Top Guns' disappear. They go on some F15 to the next pitch, and we end up with a talented young chap who is learning the ropes.

'But, but, but, where is my Tom Cruise? I liked him/her, and I want him/her on my account,' I would say.

Put the name of their Tom Cruise in the contract/agreement to be the one managing the account.

If no Tom Cruise, the agreement is null and void.

#Thisiswhatticklesme

If Tom Cruise decides to leave the agency or if he/she gets promoted, then you will have the right to select/interview the next Tom Cruise who will manage your account.

PS. This is not an agency-bashing session, just a practice that I have observed and hope to see corrected.

Post # 181

Wow!!
So many offices

#Thisiswhatticklesme

One of the first slides of an agency-pitch presentation included a map with many dots of where they have offices around the world, and I have come across many in my days.

'We are regional, we are global, we have network offices everywhere, and we can service your regional account – a piece of cake!'

Ask the pitching team a simple question:

What is the name of the managing director (MD) of another network office (at random)?

1. If they don't know (many don't), then the whole map/network thing is a hoax, a waste of time and space.

2. If you know the name of the MD, and they respond pretending to know by making a name up – *run* out the door.

PS. This is not an agency-bashing session, just a practice that I have observed on countless occasions and hope to see corrected.

Post # 182

Verbal diarrhoea

#Thisiswhatticklesme

I like to decipher messages.

TRUE STORY

I got this message from a real person (not a bot) and tried to make it into plain English so I could understand it, less the jargon and the verbal diarrhoea.

Received message:

> We must ensure clarity of our strategic direction. Our aim is to drive quality in deliverables in a consistent and timely manner, by leveraging our robust best practice knowledge. Let's align this with our team and empower them to deliver on it to our stakeholders.

I think he/she is trying to say:

#Thisiswhatticklesme

Our clear objective is to do things right, the first time, every time, and on time. Let's get the team behind this, and let's get started.

Do you agree, or have I missed anything?

Post # 183

Perspective

#Thisiswhatticklesme

I woke up this morning to hundreds of wonderful birthday messages that I was grateful for.

'Thank you'.

For my birthday, I decided to do something daring; something uncomfortable; and, of course, something exciting.

Yes, it is a bit nutty to 'Edge Walk' on the roof of the CN Tower (Toronto) at 1,168 feet above ground level, but I did it!

Perspective – I realised one thing when I was up there, looking around!
 (When I managed to open my eyes)

#Thisiswhatticklesme

- The Toronto skyline was different
- The Toronto skyline was missing something
- It felt like I was in another city

The famous CN Tower was missing.

I was *on* it!

And the view looked and felt different . . .

It made me realise the importance of perspective . . . your perspective is, and most of the time will be, different from others' even if you are in the same place.

'Deep', I know; what tickled me though was when I proudly showed this picture to my niece . . .

'Look how cool your uncle is!'

She didn't comment about my bravery, she didn't comment about how high I was, she didn't say how beautiful the view was . . .

Her first comment was:

'Ewww . . . they've got to do something with the colour of these outfits . . .'

Again, perspective!

Post # 184

Throw kindness around like confetti

#Thisiswhatticklesme

'Kindness . . . it's free . . . spread that sh$t everywhere' were the words of a friend, which resonated with me.

I was feeling a little fragile and grumpy this morning, until I saw these words on the stairs while going up for breakfast

'Throw kindness around like confetti.'

These words put a smile on my face.

I decided I was going to spread kindness around for the rest of the day.

I focused on the grumpiest people to make sure I put a smile on their face by saying something nice or making a small, kind gesture.

#Thisiswhatticklesme

My first attempt:

I went to buy my flat white coffee; the person behind the counter (Tom), had surely woken up on the wrong side of the bed!

'What do you want?' he asked without looking at me.

'Wow, perfect, this guy needs some kindness,' I thought.

I smiled and said, 'I would like a medium flat white – strong and awesome – *like you*!'

He looked up at me for the first time and smiled.

I continued, 'Please and thank you!'

He flashed another smile.

What tickled me was that the more kindness I spread, the more kindness I got back, which made me forget about my grumpiness.

Some reflection: There are many people out there who need some TLC.

Spread some kindness today!

Post # 185

Fun, action, politics, drama

#Thisiswhatticklesme

Like many of you, I have been part of many teams: project teams, functional teams, leadership teams . . .

I have experienced all kinds of team dynamics: some are fun and full of action, some are dull (yawn), and some are full of politics and drama.

Without fail, each team has been through the same four stages:

1. Forming: Coming together, excited about being assigned to be part of the team – I call this the honeymoon stage.
2. Storming: Flexing of muscles, turf marking, setting the tone, testing each other – I call this the drama stage.
3. Norming: Finding your happy place, that's when people accept, tolerate, and, most importantly, trust each other – this is the recognition stage.

#Thisiswhatticklesme

4. Performing: That's when sparks happen, people respect and understand each other's roles and strengths – and this, I call the productive stage.

These stages can happen after several months or after one meeting (depending on the maturity of the team).

And it all comes down to two essential ingredients – the right leadership and the feeling of empowerment.

What tickles me is that you know you are part of a super, fun, and performing team when you start giving each other nick names like Mary, Sharky, Cook, Weller, Imsen, Bin Bin, Sparv, Hats, Cutter, etc.

Yours sincerely,

Travis

Bonus article # 1

I am having an affair

What corporate and startup dudes and dudettes can learn from each other!

Now that I have your attention, let me share my so-called affair. I know what you're thinking . . . *No*, this is a legitimate affair, so there is nothing 9½ weeks or 50 Shades of Grey about it.

I am sitting peacefully in my office staring at my e-mails, focusing on which ones to delete and which ones are worth reading. I notice an e-mail from Kosta Petrov, CEO of P World, inviting me to speak at one of his awesome conferences. I contemplated for about 10 sec, and I accepted his invitation. So this is the 'article version' of my talk, which I recently gave at the Marketing Kingdom. The 'article version' means a much shorter version, because I know many of you, like me, can sometimes have the attention span of a goldfish.

Let's start with the definition of an affair: an affair (like any other) involves three people – you, party 1, and party 2.

#Thisiswhatticklesme

Me – A professional corporate guy with 25 years' experience with two multinational companies (the Coca-Cola Company and Tetra Pak) and an early stint in the advertising world, where I started my career.

Party 1 – of 18 years is a forward-thinking packaging and processing company that likes to go unnoticed 500 million times a day. To learn more about Party 1, where I proudly work, visit www.tetrapak.com.

Party 2 – of 2½ years is 1TAM. The first social media vlogging app, where users can express themselves and share their opinions and ideas.

So, this, I think, qualifies me to speak about both the corporate and the startup worlds. What I found and learnt through this new and serious hobby was and still is invaluable to all 'parties'.

Let me start by defining the corporate and startup worlds, as I see them. Yes, I may be generalising. (Please forgive the humour, and also forgive me if this does not apply to you.)

Corporates – with a successful and proven product or service

- Cash rich/ample resources
- Can be bureaucratic

- Homogeneous – in a corporate setting, we tend to only hire people who think like us, 'look' like us, dress like us, and, in many cases, share our values.

Startups – with a big idea

- Limited resources/shoestring budgets . . . until you secure funding
- Fast to execute/agile
- Diverse and super creative (which could sometimes be to their detriment)

Now let's look at the difference between corporate and startup *people*, who I will refer to as *Suits vs Jeans*. You know who's who.

Suits people

- Experienced/disciplined/domesticated.
- Swollen-hand syndrome, meaning: Can I do this? 'No', smack; Can I do this? 'No', smack; How about this? 'No', smack . . . and you end up with a swollen hand.
- Jargon and lots of it. To demonstrate, I took a couple of jargon words that I have heard here and there in the corporate world, and I made a sentence that sounds intelligent but actually means nothing:

#Thisiswhatticklesme

Listen buddy, I am circling back on a topic that I need your buy-in on. It's all about our core competencies that require us to look at some best-practice cases. This will certainly require us to have our ducks in a row because we simply have a burning platform here. I strongly suggest that we leverage our adjacencies and focus on our swim lane if we really want to keep our heads above water in this space. This, my friend, will move the needle on our bleeding-edge thinking. So, let's get cracking, and put our tiger team together.

Said a random corporate guy!

Suits people should:

- be open minded, challenge the status quo, in a disciplined and domesticated way.
- be curious, listen to, and learn from the startup guys . . . they have changed the world.
- drop the jargon – speak English.

Jeans people

- Wild with ideas, creative, but unstructured and make decisions on the fly.
- Do everything from licking envelopes, making coffee, to presenting in board meetings.

- Hungry and driven – they know that if 'this' doesn't work, they risk losing a lot – high risk and living from day to day.

Jeans people should:

- be prepared to be rejected, sometimes several times a day, and don't let that discourage you . . . (I hope).
- don't accept 'No' for an answer – put yourself forward, knock on every possible door, even if it is your mother-in-law.
- take happy pills, you will need them; be humble, and be super patient – you will need both, the pills and the patience.

What I learnt as a corporate dude

- To find your passion early (I am no longer a 26-year-old 'spring chicken').
- Learn to spot talent, that sparkle in their eyes – as diverse as they may come – even if they have ponytails and wear yellow jeans.
- Nurture, build, and use both your experience and contacts – actively, not just when you need them.
- Cross-fertilise (jargon alert) ideas and experiences. For example, our digital communications agenda in my corporate job has changed dramatically, thanks to my newly acquired knowledge.

I know I rambled on, but there are three things I want you to remember from this article:

1. Speak English – simple is the new cool.
2. The corporate world can be the new breeding ground for young startup people.
3. Give startups a chance.

Bonus article # 2

1+1 doesn't always = 2

A little lesson about negotiations, the Chinese way.

As written by Marc Wright a couple of years back!

Let me introduce you to a good friend of mine, Khaled Ismail, Corporate Brand Director at Tetra Pak. Last night we were enjoying the sights of Shanghai's famous waterfront – The Bund – when Khaled came across a street vendor selling come cute blobby toys (a ball of water in rubber that squashes itself when thrown and then gradually unsticks and reforms in an amusing manner). Khaled decided to buy 3 for his children and then told me to observe how to bargain.

Khaled: How Much?

Street Vendor: 10 Yuan each.

Khaled: I'll take these 3 for 10 Yuan.

#Thisiswhatticklesme

Street Vendor: 10 Yuan each?

Khaled: No 10 Yuan for all 3.

Street Vendor: %**&£$$!!

At which point, Khaled walks away. Inevitably the vendor chases after him and Khaled returns reluctantly.

Street Vendor: OK I'll sell you 3 for 20 Yuan.

Khaled: No, I'll tell you what I'm going to pay, and the price is going down.

6 Yuan for all 3.

Khaled then walks again – he virtually runs along the pier. Of course, the vendor chases after him and sells him 3 at just 2 Yuan each.

We stroll on further and Khaled explains the golden rule.

'You have to be prepared to walk away at any point in the negotiation. He knew I wanted them, but he also knew that only I had the choice to walk away – so the onus was on him. Effectively, he ended up bartering with himself.'

Khaled M. Ismail

As we returned along the walkway, we re-passed the street vendor who was selling some more toys at 10 Yuan.

Quick as a flash, Khaled sat down beside him and started offering the three he had just bought at the knock-down price of 5 Yuan each. Fortunately for Khaled's kids (and the hapless vendor), our car turned up to whisk him away to the airport. But not before he got a round of applause from an assembled crowd of Chinese celebrating his trading skills.

I suddenly had a renewed respect (and no little sympathy) for my colleagues, in simply-experience who, every quarter, have to renegotiate contracts with Tetra Pak.

Marc

Bonus article #3

Work/life balance with a sprinkle of tough love

Forgive me for being a little provocative, with a sprinkle of tough love!

What's all the fuss with the work/life balance nonsense that I keep hearing about? Here are my two-and-a-half cents:

If you are someone who hates his/her job, drops everything at five o'clock and runs home, then you should quit and look for another job immediately.

Work shouldn't be a miserable affair. If it is for you, find something that makes you want to wake up and run to 'work', to that something that you do for over 60 per cent of your adult life. Find something that makes you happy. Work/deal only with people who appreciate and respect you, your commitment, and your talent. Drop the rest, avoid them, delete them – or in the new millennial terminology, 'block' or 'unfriend' them from your life.

When I see a chart like this (below), I question whether our dear millennials want to actually work. Of the top three important factors of their focus on finding a job, 41.2 per cent has nothing to do with the actual job. Then they want a sense of meaning, and professional training programmes . . . Do I get a sense of 'entitlement' here? Maybe I am wrong.

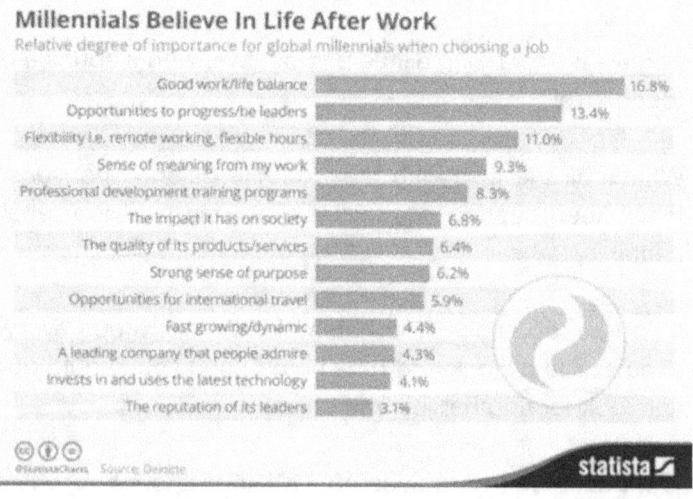

Work doesn't have to mean going to a depressing office; sitting in a nasty, uncomfortable chair; staring at a lifeless screen; or dreading the idea of serving another demanding customer. It doesn't. I would hate it too.

And if sitting by the beach, staring at the sea, and counting sand grains is what you want in life, because that is what 'balance' means to you, do it, just don't expect or feel entitled to the big salary or the next promotion.

Don't be needy; you are entitled to nothing you don't deserve or work hard for.

I hear people talk about having a job – 'it's just a job' – that 'pays the bills'. Then guess what? That is what it is. Do your job, pay the bills, stop whining about work/life balance, and continue to pursue what you love until you find it.

If you do something you love with people you enjoy working and being with, then the concept of this 'work/life balance' myth disappears.

Try it!

Tell me what tickles you. This would inspire me to write more, and I will mention you as a contributor.

If you have a story to tell, you know what to do:

khaledismail@me.com

#Thisiswhatticklesme

www.thisiswhatticklesme.com

www.ingramcontent.com/pod-product-compliance
Lightning Source LLC
Chambersburg PA
CBHW071853290426
44110CB00013B/1126